Collins
gem

Collins
Czech
phrasebook

Consultant
Michaela Čaňková

First published 1996
This edition published 2007
Copyright © HarperCollins Publishers
Reprint 10 9 8 7 6 5 4 3 2 1 0
Typeset by Davidson Pre-Press, Glasgow
Printed in Malaysia by Imago

www.collins.co.uk

ISBN 13 978-0-00-724666-3
ISBN 10 0-00-724666-8

Using your phrasebook

Your *Collins Gem Phrasebook* is designed to help you locate the exact phrase you need, when you need it, whether on holiday or for business. If you want to adapt the phrases, you can easily see where to substitute your own words using the dictionary section, and the clear, full-colour layout gives you direct access to the different topics.

The Gem Phrasebook includes:
• Over 70 topics arranged thematically. Each phrase is accompanied by a simple pronunciation guide which eliminates any problems pronouncing foreign words.

• A Top ten tips section to safeguard against any cultural faux pas, giving essential dos and don'ts for situations involving local customs or etiquette.

• Practical hints to make your stay trouble free, showing you where to go and what to do when dealing with everyday matters such as travel or hotels and offering valuable tourist information.

• Face to face sections so that you understand what is being said to you. These example mini-dialogues give you a good idea of what to expect from a real conversation.

- Common announcements and messages you may hear, ensuring that you never miss the important information you need to know when out and about.

- A clearly laid-out 3000-word dictionary means you will never be stuck for words.

- A basic grammar section which will enable you to build on your phrases.

- A list of public holidays to avoid being caught out by unexpected opening and closing hours, and to make sure you don't miss the celebrations!

It's worth spending time before you embark on your travels just looking through the topics to see what is covered and becoming familiar with what might be said to you.

Whatever the situation, your *Gem Phrasebook* is sure to help!

Contents

Pronouncing Czech

Czech contains some unfamiliar letters and a few difficult sounds for English speakers. The letters **b d f g h k l m n p s t v x** and **z** sound the same as in English. Note that **g** is always hard as in 'lag', never soft as in 'large', and **s** is always hissed as in 'less', never like z as in 'Les'. The stress is always on the first syllable of the word. The pronunciation guide in this book uses hyphens to separate the syllables. The letters **l** and **r** can be a syllable in their own right, e.g. **Vltava** (vl-ta-va), **sprcha** (sprr-kha), and **h** is always pronounced, even at the end of a word, e.g. **pstruh** (pstroo-h). See ALPHABET for a full list of the pronunciation symbols we use.

Consonants	
c	is pronounced like 'ts' in 'bi**ts**', not like 'k' or 's'
č	is pronounced like 'ch' in '**ch**urch'
ch	(considered a separate letter) is pronounced like the rasping 'ch' in the Scottish word 'lo**ch**', not like 'ch' in 'church'
š	is pronounced like 'sh' in '**sh**ut'
j	is pronounced like 'y' in '**y**es'
d'	is something like the sound in 'le**d y**ou'; we show this in the pronuciation guide with a small raised y, e.g. **ted'** (ted^y)

7

t'	is something like the sound in 'le**t y**ou', e.g. **let'** (letʸ)
ň	is pronounced like 'ni' in 'o**ni**on', e.g. **Plzeň** pl-zenʸ
ř	is an unusual sound combining rolled 'r' and 'zh', e.g. **Dvořák** (dvo-ʳzhak). If you can't manage it, try saying 'zh' instead.

Vowels

a	is pronounced as in f**a**t, not as in f**a**te
e	is pronounced as in p**e**t, not as in P**e**te
i	is pronounced as in p**i**ll, not as in p**i**le
o	is pronounced as in p**o**p, not as in p**o**pe
u	is pronounced like 'oo' in 'b**oo**k', not as in t**u**b or t**u**be
y	is pronounced as in h**i**ll, not as in **y**eti

Vowels can be long or short. When the vowel is long, shown in Czech by an accent (e.g. **ú** or **ů**), we highlight it in bold, i.e. **tabák** ta-b**a**k. You will also see combinations of vowels such as **au** (aᵂ) and **ou** (oᵂ), like '**ou**ch' and 'c**oa**ch' respectively.

Top ten tips

• •

1 Czechs remove their shoes when entering a home and leave them outside.

2 The Czech Republic has a zero-tolerance policy on alcohol consumption, so even a single beer before driving could get you into trouble.

3 Always wait to be invited to use somebody's first name.

4 If you receive a gift, you should open it immediately and in front of the giver.

5 Acknowledge people in lifts, train compartments and shop counters by saying, '**dobrý den**' (hello) and '**nashledanou**' (goodbye).

6 Avoid hailing a taxi in the street. It's best to phone a taxi firm and make sure the driver turns on the meter.

7 In restaurants, expect to sit with other people if there is space – others will sit with you. Always ask for permission first.

8 When giving flowers, always give them in odd numbers. Even numbers are given at funerals.

9 Most Czechs know which mushrooms to pick in the woods and are prepared to get up at 4 o'clock in the morning to do so. Picking mushrooms is the Czech national passion.

10 Most people leave for their '**chata**' (a weekend house in the country) on Friday afternoon and come back on Sunday evening. This means that Prague is empty of locals at weekends and heavy traffic should be expected going out of and into Prague on these days.

Talking to people

Hello/goodbye, yes/no

In 1993 Czechoslovakia (**Československo**) split into the Czech Republic (**Česká Republika**), comprising Bohemia (**Čechy**) and Moravia (**Morava**), and Slovakia (**Slovensko**). The adjective **český** refers either generally to both the Czech lands or specifically to Bohemia. The Slovak language is different from Czech, but Czech will be understood in Slovakia.

Yes	**Ano**	
	a-no	
No	**Ne**	
	ne	
Excuse me/ sorry/pardon?	**Promiňte**	
	pro-minY-te	
Please/you're welcome	**Prosím**	
	pro-s**ee**m	
Thank you	**Děkuji**	
	dYe-koo-yi	

Thanks	**Díky** d**ee**-ki
Hi/bye (informal)	**Ahoj** a-hoy
Hello (formal)	**Dobrý den** dob-r**ee** den
Goodbye (formal)	**Nashledanou** nas-hle-da-no^w
Good morning	**Dobré ráno** dob-r**e** r**a**-no
Mr...	**Pane...** p**a**-ne...
Mrs/Ms...	**Paní...** pa-n**ee**...
Miss...	**Slečno...** slech-no...
Good evening	**Dobrý večer** dob-r**ee** ve-cher
Goodnight	**Dobrou noc** dob-ro^w nots
How are you? (formal)	**Jak se máte?** yak se m**a**-te?
Fine, thanks	**Dobře, děkuji** dob-^rzhe, d^ye-koo-yi
and you?	**a vy?** a vi?
How are you? (informal)	**Jak se máš?** yak se m**a**sh?

12

(informal)	**A ty?**
	a ti?
I don't speak Czech	**Nemluvím česky**
	nem-loo-**vee**m ches-ki
I don't understand	**Nerozumím**
	ne-ro-zoo-m**ee**m

Key phrases

Do you have...?	**Máte...?**
	m**a**-te...?
any bread	**chleba**
	khle-ba
any milk	**mléko**
	ml**e**-ko
How much is it?	**Kolik to stojí?**
	Ko-lik to sto-y**ee**?
this one	**toto**
	to-to
that one	**tamto**
	tam-to
When...?	**Kdy...?**
	kdi...?
At what time...?	**V kolik hodin...?**
	vko-lik ho-din...?

13

Today	**Dnes**
	dnes
Tomorrow	**Zítra**
	z**ee**-tra
How many?	**Kolik?**
	ko-lik?
Which one?	**Který?**
	kte-r**ee**?
Where is...?	**Kde je...?**
	kde ye...?
Where are...?	**Kde jsou...?**
	kde yso^w...?
Where are the toilets?	**Kde jsou toalety?**
	kde yso^w to-a-le-ti?
How do I get to...?	**Jak se dostanu do/na...?**
	yak se dos-ta-noo do/na...?
to the station	**na nádraží**
	na n**a**d-ra-zh**ee**
to the centre	**do centra**
	do tsen-tra
Where is...?	**Kde to je?**
	kde to ye?
Is it far?	**Je to daleko?**
	ye to da-le-ko?
I don't want it	**Nechci to**
	nekh-tsi to
Can I...?	**Mohu/Můžu...?**
	mo-hoo/m**oo**-zhoo...?

Polite expressions

In the Czech Republic people greet each other **dobrý den** dob-r**ee** den or **ahoj** a-hoy (informal for BOTH 'hi' and 'bye').

How do you do?/ Pleased to meet you	**Těší mě** t^ye-sh**ee** mn^ye
This is my husband	**To je můj muž** to ye m**oo**y moozh
This is my wife	**To je moje žena** to ye mo-ye zhe-na
This is a gift for you	**Tady je dárek pro vás** ta-di ye d**a**-rek pro v**a**s
The meal was delicious	**Jídlo bylo skvělé** yid-lo bi-lo skv^ye-le
Thank you very much	**Děkujeme moc** d^ye-koo-ye-me mots
Enjoy your holiday!	**Hezkou dovolenou!** hez-ko^w do-vo-le-no^w!
I'd like to wish you... (formal)	**Rád(a) bych vám popřál(a)...** r**a**d(a) bikh v**a**m pop-ʳzh**a**l(a)...
(informal)	**Rád(a) bych ti popřál(a)...** r**a**d(a) bikh ti pop-ʳzh**a**l(a)...

Can we...?	**Můžeme...?** m**oo**-zhe-me...?
Is it...?	**Je to...?** ye to...?
Are they...?	**Jsou...?** yso^w...?
Can I smoke?	**Mohu si zapálit?** moo-hoo si za-p**a**-lit?
Who?	**Kdo?** kdo?
What?	**Co?** tso?
Why?	**Proč?** proch?
How?	**Jak?** yak?
I'd like...	**Chci...** khtsi...
I'd like pasta	**Chci těstoviny** khtsi t^yes-to-vi-ni
I'd like an ice cream	**Chci zmrzlinu** khtsi zmrr-zli-noo
We'd like...	**Chceme...** khtse-me...
We'd like two cakes	**Chceme dva dorty** khtse-me dva dor-ti
More...	**Ještě...** yesh-t^ye...

More bread	**Ještě chleba**
	yesh-tYe khle-ba
More water	**Ještě vodu**
	yesh-tYe vo-doo
Another...	**Ještě jednou...**
	yesh-tYe yed-no^w...
Another coffee	**Ještě jednu kávu**
	yesh-tYe yed-noo k**a**-voo
Another beer	**Ještě jedno pivo**
	yesh-tYe yed-no pi-vo
large	**velký**
	vel-k**ee**
small	**malý**
	ma-l**ee**
It doesn't matter	**to nevadí**
	to ne-va-d**ee**

Signs and notices

muži/páni	gentlemen
dámy/ženy	ladies
otevřeno	open
zavřeno	closed
tam	push
sem	pull

pokladna	cash desk/ticket offic
oddělení úrazů	A&E/casualty
první pomoc	first aid
plno/plný	full
záchody/toalety	toilets
volno	vacant/free
obsazeno	occupied
nefunguje	out of order
suterén	basement
Přízemí	ground floor
vchod	entrance
první patro	first floor
vstup zakázán	no entry
vchod	exit
nouzový východ	emergency exit
obsazeno	no vacancies
koupání zakázáno	no swimming
k vlaku	to the train
Nástupiště	platform
plať te u pokladny	pay at cash desk
úschovna zavazadel	left luggage
koupelna	bathroom
zákaz	...forbidden/no...
nebezpečí	danger
slevy	reductions
informace	information
nekuřáci	non-smoking

Happy Birthday!	**Všechno nejlepší k narozeninám!**
	vshekh-no ney-lep-sh**ee** k na-ro-ze-ni-n**a**m!
Cheers!	**Na zdraví!**
	na zdra-v**ee**!
Congratulations!	**Blahopřeji!**
	bla-hop-ʳzhe-yi!
Have a good trip!	**Šťastnou cestu!**
	shtʸas-tnoʷ tses-too!
Welcome	**Vítejte**
	v**ee**-tey-te
(reply to this)	**děkuji**
	dʸe-koo-yi
Bon appetit	**Dobrou chuť**
	dob-roʷ khootʸ
(reply to this)	**děkuji**
	dʸe-koo-yi

Celebrations

• •

Happy New Year!	**Šťastný Nový rok!**
	shtʸas-tn**ee** no-v**ee** rok!
Happy Easter!	**Veselé Velikonoce!**
	ve-se-l**e** ve-li-ko-no-tse!

Merry Christmas!	**Veselé Vánoce!**
	ve-se-**le** va-no-tse!
Bon appetit	**Dobrou chut'**
	dob-ro^w khoot^Y
Thank you (reply	**děkuji**
to 'Bon Appetit')	d^Ye-koo-yi

Making friends

• •

There are two ways of addressing people: informal
and formal. In this section we have used the
informal form.

FACE TO FACE

A Jak se jmenuješ?
yak se yme-noo-yesh?
What is your name?

B Jmenuji se...
yme-noo-yi se...
My name is...

A Kde bydlíš?
kde bid-**lee**sh?
Where do you live?

B Bydlím v Londýně
bid-**lee**m v lon-**dee**-n^Ye
I live in London

A **Jak se ti tady líbí?**
yak se ti ta-di l**ee**-b**ee**?
How do you like it here?

B **Moc**
mots
It's great

I'm from England	**Jsem z Anglie**	
	ysem zang-gli-ye	
I'm from Australia	**Jsem z Austrálie**	
	ysem za^ws-tr**a**-li-ye	
This is...	**To je...**	
	to ye...	
my friend (male)	**můj přítel**	
	m**oo**y p^rzh**ee**-tel	
my friend (female)	**moje přítelkyně**	
	mo-ye p^rzh**ee**-tel-ki-nye	
my son	**můj syn**	
	m**oo**y sin	
my husband	**můj manžel**	
	m**oo**y man-zhel	
my wife	**moje manželka**	
	mo-ye man-zhel-ka	
my daughter	**moje dcera**	
	mo-ye dtse-ra	
I have children	**Mám děti**	
	m**a**m d^ye-ti	
I have no children	**Nemám děti**	
	ne-m**a**m d^ye-ti	

Making friends

> Leisure /Interests (p 70) **> Sport** (p 77)   21

Work

What do you do?	**Jaké je tvoje zaměstnání?**
	ya-ke ye tvo-ye za-mnᵉest-na-nee?
Do you enjoy it?	**Líbí se vám to?**
	lee-bee se vam to?
I'm...	**Jsem...**
	ysem...
a doctor	**doktor(ka)**
	dok-tor(-ka)
a teacher	**učitel(-ka)**
	oo-chi-tel(-ka)

YOU MAY HEAR...

Podnikám	I'm self-employed
pod-ni-kam	
Jsem na volné noze	I'm freelance
ysem na vol-ne no-ze	

Weather

It's sunny	**Svítí slunce**
	svee-tee sloon-tse
It's raining	**Prší**
	prr-shee

It's snowing	**Sněží**
	snYe-zh**ee**
It's windy	**Je vítr**
	ye v**ee**-trr
What is the weather forecast for tomorrow?	**Jaká je předpověď počasí na zítřek?**
	ya-k**a** ye p^rzhed-po-v^yedy po-cha-s**ee** na z**ee**t-^rzhek?
What's the temperature?	**Jaká je teplota?**
	ya-k**a** ye tep-lo-ta?
It is very hot	**Je hrozné horko**
	ye hroz-n**e** hor-ko
I am hot/cold	**Je mi horko/zima**
	ye mi hor-ko/zi-ma
Will there be a storm?	**Bude bouřka?**
	boo-de bo^wrzh-ka?
What beautiful weather!	**To je krásné počasí!**
	to ye kr**a**s-n**e** po-cha-s**ee**!
What awful weather!	**To je hrozné počasí!**
	to ye hroz-n**e** po-cha-s**ee**!

Weather

YOU MAY HEAR...

| **Myslím, že bude pršet** | I think it will rain |
| mis-l**ee**m zhe boo-de prr-shet | |

Getting around

Asking the way

• •

If you want to ask directions in the street, start with **Promiňte** (excuse me!).

vpravo vpra-vo	right
vlevo vle-vo	left
rovně rov-nʸe	straight on
vedle ved-le	next to
blízko bleez-ko	near
naproti na-pro-ti	opposite
křižovatka kʳzhi-zho-vat-ka	crossroads
semafor se-ma-for	traffic lights
most most	bridge
náměstí na-mnʸes-tee	square
roh roh	corner

FACE TO FACE

A **Promiňte, jak se dostanu na nádraží?**
pro-min^y-te yak se dos-ta-noo na n**a**d-ra-zh**ee**?
Excuse me, how do I get to the station?

B **Pořád rovně, za kostelem doleva**
po-^rzhad rov-ne za kos-te-lem do-le-va
Keep straight on, after the church turn left

A **Je to daleko?**
ye to da-le-ko?
Is it far?

B **Asi deset minut**
asi de-set mi-nut
About ten minutes

A **Děkuji**
d^ye-koo-yi
Thank you

B **Prosím**
pro-s**ee**m
You're welcome

Where is…?	**Kde je…?**
	kde ye…?
We're lost	**Zabloudili jsme**
	zab-lo^w-di-li ysme
I don't know how to get to…	**Nevím, jak se dostanu na/do…**
	ne-v**ee**m yak se dos-ta-noo na/do…
Is this the right way?	**Jdu správně?**
	y-doo spr**a**v-n^ye?

Asking the way

25

Can we walk there?	**Dá se tam jít pěšky?**
	da se tam yeet pYesh-ki?
Can you show me on the map?	**Můžete mi to ukázat na mapě?**
	moo-zhe-te mi to oo-ka-zat na ma-pYe?

Bus and coach

• •

On Fridays and before public holidays, it is advisable to buy tickets in advance from the bus station. You can buy tickets for local transport from tobacconists, kiosks, vending machines, etc. They are valid for all forms of public transport.

Jízdenka/lístek	ticket
yeez-den-ka/lístek	
autobusové nádraží	coach station
aʷ-to-boos-o-ve na-dra-zhee	
místenka mees-ten-ka	reservation

FACE TO FACE

A Promiňte, který autobus jede do centra?
pro-miny-te kte-r**ee** a^W-to-boos ye-de do tsen-tra?
Which bus goes to the centre?

B Osmnáctka
O-soom-n**a**tst-ka
Number 18

A Kde je zastávka?
kde ye zas-t**a**v-ka?
Where is the bus stop?

B Tam
tam
Over there

A Kde se kupují lístky?
kde se koo-poo-y**ee** l**ee**st-ki?
Where can I buy tickets?

B V novinovém stanku
v no-vi-no-v**e**m stan-koo
At the news stand

I am going to…	**Chci jet do/na…**
	khtsi yet do/na…
to the airport	**na letiště**
	na le-t^yish-t^ye
to the centre	**do centra**
	do tsen-tra
Is there a bus to…?	**Jezdí autobus do…?**
	yez-d**ee** a^W-to-boos do…?

Bus and coach

Where is the coach station?	**Kde je autobusové nádraží?**
	kde ye a^w-to-boo-so-ve na-dra-zhee?
How frequent are the buses to...?	**Jak často jezdí autobusy do...?**
	yak chas-to yez-dee a^w-to-boo-si do...?
When is the first/ last bus to...?	**Kdy jede první/poslední autobus do...?**
	kdi ye-de prrv-nee/pos-led-nee a^w-to-boos do?
Where's the timetable?	**Kde je jízdní řád?**
	kde ye yeezd-nee ʳzhad?
Where do I get off?	**Kde mám vystoupit?**
	kde mam vis-to^w-pit?

Metro

. . . .

Prague is the only Czech city with a metro system. Its three metro lines run from 5am until midnight every day. There are no zones. There are tickets at two prices, each valid for one time-limited journey in one direction, including changes. The more expensive ticket enables you to use more than one mode of transport (metro, tram and bus). You must validate your ticket by stamping it in a machine on entering the metro, tram or bus.

> **Luggage** (p 91)

Where is the metro station?	**Kde je stanice metra?**
	kde ye sta-ni-tse met-ra?
I am going to...	**Jedu do...**
	ye-doo do...
How do I get to...?	**Jak se dostanu do...?**
	yak se dos-ta-noo do...?
Which line is it?	**Která linka je to?**
	kte-r**a** lin-ka ye to?
One ticket for twenty crowns	**Jednu jízdenku za dvacet**
	yed-nu **yee**z-den-ku za dva-tset
Excuse me!	**Promiňte!**
	pro-min^y-te!
I'm getting off here	**Vystupuji tady**
	vis-too-poo-yi ta-di

YOU MAY HEAR...

Můstek, příští stanice... m**oo**s-tek, p^rzh**ee**-sht**ee** sta-ni-tse...	Next stop...

Metro

Train

....

There are two types of train, slow (**osobní**) and faster ones (**rychlík, expres** and **spěšný**). International trains and some express trains are designated as **Intercity**, **Eurocity** or **Supercity**. A supplement is payable on these trains. Train travel is much cheaper in the Czech Republic than in the West, and children under 15 pay half price. Food and drink can be bought in dining cars on long-distance trains. Be sure to make a reservation (**místenka**) when travelling on public holidays or at weekends.

nádraží na-dra-zh**ee**	station
vlak vlak	train
nástupiště na-stoo-pish-t^Ye	platform
zpoždění (on train noticeboards) zpozh-d^Ye-**nee**	delay
pokladna po-klad-na	booking office
jízdní řád y**ee**zd-n**ee** ⸢zh**a**d	timetable
spojení spo-ye-n**ee**	connection
osobní vlak o-sob-n**ee** vlak	passenger train
rychlík rikh-l**ee**k	fast/express train

> **Luggage** (p 91)

A **Tři jízdenky do...**
třzhi yeez-den-ki do...
I'd like 3 tickets to...

B **Tam nebo zpáteční?**
tam ne-bo zpa-tech-nee?
Single or return?

Where is the station?	**Kde je nádraží?** kde ye nad-ra-zhee?
1 single	**jednou** yed-no^w
2 singles	**dvakrát** dva-krat
to...	**do...** do...
1 return	**zpáteční** zpa-tech-nee
2 returns	**dva zpáteční** dva zpa-tech-nee
to...	**do...** do...
2 adults	**dva celé** dva tse-le
1 adult and 2 children	**jeden celý a dva poloviční** ye-den tse-lee a dva po-lo-vich-nee
I want to make a reservation	**Chci si koupit místenku** khtsi si ko^w-pit mees-ten-koo

Train

31

first class	**první třídu**
	prrv-n**ee** t^rzh**ee**-doo
second class	**druhou třídu**
	droo-ho^w t^rzh**ee**-doo
Is there a supplement to pay?	**Je nějaký příplatek?**
	ye n^ye-ya-k**ee** p^rzh**ee**-pla-tek?
When is the next train?	**Kdy jede další vlak?**
	kdi ye-de dal-sh**ee** vlak?
to Brno	**do Brna**
	do brr-na
Which platform?	**Ze kterého nástupiště?**
	ze kte-r**e**-ho n**a**s-too-pish-t^ye?
When does it arrive?	**Kdy to přijede?**
	kdi to p^rzhi-ye-de?
in Brno	**do Brna**
	do brr-na
What time does it leave?	**V kolik hodin to odjíždí?**
	vko-lik ho-din to od-y**ee**zh-d**ee**?
At what time?	**V kolik hodin?**
	vko-lik ho-din?
Do I have to change?	**Musím přesedat?**
	moo-s**ee**m p^rzhe-se-dat?
Where?	**Kde?**
	kde?
Is this the train...?	**Je toto vlak...?**
	ye to-to vlak...?
for Brno	**do Brna**
	do br-na

Excuse me (to get by)	**S dovolením**
	s do-vo-le-n**ee**m
Is this seat free?	**Je tady volno?**
	ye ta-di vol-no?

Taxi

••••••••••••••••••••••••••••••••

Only get into yellow cars displaying the sign **AAA**.
Make sure the driver switches on the meter when
you get in and keep an eye on the total fare. Ask for
a receipt. Prague taxi drivers are known to over-
charge, and foreign visitors are an easy target. It is
often safer to phone 14014 for a taxi from a hotel or
restaurant than to get into one on the street.

Where can I get a taxi?	**Kde najdu taxi?**
	kde nay-doo tak-si?
I want to go to...	**Chci jet do/na...**
	khtsi yet do/na...
to the coach station	**na autobusové nádraží**
	na a^w-to-boo-so-v**e** n**a**d-ra-zh**ee**
to the city centre	**do centra města**
	do tsen-tra mn^Yes-ta
How much is it...?	**Kolik to stojí...?**
	ko-lik to sto-y**ee**...?

Getting around

to this address	**na tuto adresu**
	na too-to ad-re-soo
to the airport	**na letiště**
	na le-tish-tʸe
Please stop here	**Zastavte tady, prosím**
	zas-tav-te ta-di, pro-s**ee**m
Please wait	**Počkejte, prosím**
	poch-key-te, pro-s**ee**m
I'd like a receipt	**Dejte mi, prosím, potvrzení**
	dey-te mi, pro-s**ee**m
	pot-vrr-ze-n**ee**
Keep the change	**Nechte si drobné**
	nekh-te si drob-n**e**
Switch on the meter, please	**Zapněte taxametr, prosím**
	zap-nʸe-te tak-sa-me-trr,
	pro-s**ee**m
It is too expensive	**To je příliš drahé**
	to ye pʳzh**ee**-lish dra-h**e**
This is more than on the meter	**To je víc než na taxametru**
	to ye v**ee**ts nezh na tak-sa-met-roo
I'm in a hurry	**Pospíchám**
	pos-p**ee**-kh**a**m

Tram

Prague has an extensive tram network. Trams operate from 5am to midnight, with some 'night trams' running after midnight. Generally, trams run on time (see the timetables at tram stops). Tickets (also valid for buses and metro) are available from kiosks, tobacconists' and ticket machines.

When is the tram to...?	**Kdy jede tramvaj do...?**
	kdi ye-de tram-vay do...?
Is this the right tram to...?	**Jede tahle tramvaj do...?**
	ye-de ta-hle tram-vay do...?

YOU MAY HEAR...

| **Musíte přestoupit** | You have to change |
| mu-**see**-te p^rzhe-sto^w-pit | |

Air travel

Most signs are in English as well as Czech. Prague has its Ruzyně international airport and most large cities have their local airports, too (also served by charter flights). There are buses from the airport to Prague city centre.

letiště	le-tish-t^ye	airport
přílety	p^rzhee-le-ti	arrivals
odlety	od-le-ti	departures
vnitrostátní vni-tro-st**a**t-n**ee**		domestic
mezinárodní me-zi-n**a**-rod-n**ee**		international
(číslovaný) východ (ch**ee**s-lo-va-n**ee**) v**ee**-khod		gate
zpoždění zpo-zhd^ye-n**ee**		delay

To the airport, please	**Na letiště, prosím**	na le-t^yish-t^ye, pro-s**ee**m
How much is it to the airport?	**Kolik to stojí na letiště?**	ko-lik to sto-y**ee** na le-t^yish-t^ye?
My flight is at... o'clock	**Odlétám v ... hodin**	od-l**e**-t**a**m v ... ho-din
Is there a bus to the airport?	**Jezdí na letiště autobus?**	yez-d**ee** na le-t^yish-t^ye a^w-to-boos?
into town	**do města**	do mn^yes-ta
I want to reconfirm my flight	**Chci potvrdit let**	khtsi pot-vrr-dit let
to London	**do Londýna**	do lon-d**ee**-na
to Glasgow	**do Glasgow**	do glas-gow

> **Luggage** (p 91)

Běžte okamžitě k východu číslo bYezh-te o-kam-zhi-tYe kvee-kho-doo chees-lo...	Go immediately to gate number...
Let ... je opožděn let ... ye o-pozh-dYen	Flight ... is delayed

Customs control

....

pas pas	passport
celní kontrola tsel-nee kon-tro-la	customs control

Do I have to pay duty on this?	**Musím za to platit clo?** moo-seem za to pla-tit tslo?
It is a gift	**To je dárek** to ye da-rek
I bought this in Britain	**To jsem koupil(a) v Británii** to ysem koW-pil(a) v bri-ta-ni-yi
It is my medicine	**To je můj lék** to ye mooy lek

Driving

Car hire

The major car hire firms can be found at Prague airport or in the city centre. For addresses consult Yellow Pages. UK driving licence holders do not require an international driving licence, but the minimum driving age is 21. You need a credit card to pay the big firms; small local firms are usually much cheaper.

klíče kl**ee**-che	keys
doklady o pojištění auta do-kla-di o po-yish-t^Ye-n**ee** a^W-ta	insurance documents
řidičský průkaz ^rzhi-dich-sk**ee** pr**oo**-kaz	driving licence

I want to hire a car

Chci si pronajmout auto
khtsi si pro-nay-mo^wt a^w-to

Where can I hire a car?

Kde si mohu pronajmout auto?
kde si mo-hoo pro-nay-mo^wt a^w-to?

a small car	**malé auto**
	ma-l**e** a^w-to
a large car	**velké auto**
	vel-k**e** a^w-to
with air	**s klimatizací**
conditioning	s kli-ma-ti-za-ts**ee**
automatic	**s automatickou**
	převodovkou
	s au-to-ma-tits-ko^w
	p^rzhe-vo-dov-ko^w
Is there a deposit	**Mám zaplatit zálohu?**
to pay?	m**a**m zap-la-tit z**a**-lo-hoo?
Is insurance	**Je pojištění zahrnuto v**
included?	**ceně?**
	ye po-yish-t^ye-n**ee** za-hrr-noo-to v
	tse-n^ye?
Is there a charge	**Platí se podle kilometrů?**
per kilometre?	pla-t**ee** se pod-le ki-lo-met-r**oo**?
I'd like to return	**Rád bych to auto vrátil v...**
it to...	r**a**d bikh to a^w-to vr**a**-til v...

Car hire

Auto vraťte s plnou	Please return the car
nádrží	with a full tank
a^w-to vrat^y-te spl-no^w	
n**a**dr-zh**ee**	

Driving

• •

The main road signs are international and the
speed limits are: motorway – 130 km/h; built-up
areas – 50 km/h; other roads – 90 km/h. Police will
impose on-the-spot fines for violations. No alcohol
consumption is allowed when driving in the Czech
Republic. To use motorways you must display a
windscreen sticker (**dálniční nálepka**), sold for
a small sum at the border, petrol stations or post
offices. All cars must be equipped with a first-aid
kit, reflective vest and warning triangle, and drivers
must carry a valid driving licence and vehicle
registration document. Headlights must be used
at all times.

Can I park here?	**Mohu zde zaparkovat?**
	mo-hoo zde za-par-ko-vat?
For how long?	**Jak dlouho?**
	yak dlo^w-ho?
Where can I park?	**Kde mohu zaparkovat?**
	kde mo-hoo za-par-ko-vat?
Do I need snow chains?	**Potřebuji sněhové řetězy?**
	pot-ʳzhe-boo-yi sn^ye-ho-v**e** ʳzhe-t^ye-zy?

Váš řidičský průkaz vash ⌐zhi-dich-sk**ee** pr**oo**-kaz	Your driving licence
Tady nesmíte parkovat ta-di nes-m**ee**-te par-ko-vat	You can't park here

Petrol

• •

There are plenty of petrol stations, some open 24 hours a day. They are self-service and often have a shop and toilets. They take credit cards as well as cash.

čerpací stanice cher-pa-ts**ee** sta-ni-tse	petrol station
benzin ben-zin	petrol
nafta naf-ta	diesel
bezolovnatý benzin/ **natural** bez-o-lov-na-t**ee** ben-zin/ na-too-ral	unleaded petrol

Where is the nearest petrol station?	**Kde je nejbližší čerpací stanice?** kde ye ney-blizh-sh**ee** cher-pa-ts**ee** sta-ni-tse?

41

U kterého stojanu jste tankoval?	Which pump did you use?
oo kte-**re**-ho sto-ya-noo yste tan-ko-val?	
Nemáme...	We have no...
ne-**ma**-me...	

Breakdown

If your car breaks down, you should use a breakdown triangle. ÚAMK is the Czech equivalent to the AA, dial 1230. Garages tend to specialize in particular makes of car.

My car has broken down	Moje auto má poruchu
	mo-ye a^w-to m**a** po-roo-khoo
Can you help me?	Můžete mi pomoct?
	m**oo**-zhe-te mi po-motst?
I've run out of petrol	Došel mi benzin
	do-shel mi ben-zin
The battery is flat	Mám vybitou baterii
	m**a**m vi-bi-to^w ba-te-ri-yi
The engine won't start	Nemohu nastartovat
	ne-mo-hoo nas-tar-to-vat

42

I don't know what's wrong	**Nevím, co s tím je** ne-**vee**m tso st**ee**m ye	
I have a flat tyre	**Mám píchlou pneumatiku** m**a**m p**ee**-khlo^W pne^W-ma-ti-koo	
Where is the nearest garage?	**Kde je nejbližší autoservis?** kde ye ney-blizh-sh**ee** a^W-to-ser-vis?	
How long will it take?	**Jak dlouho to bude trvat?** yak dlo^W-ho to boo-de trr-vat?	
How much will it cost?	**Kolik to bude stát?** ko-lik to boo-de st**a**t?	

Car parts

• •

The ... doesn't work	**... nefunguje** ... ne-foon-goo-ye	
The ... don't work	**... nefungují** ... ne-foon-goo-y**ee**	

accelerator	**plyn**	plin
alternator	**alternátor**	al-ter-n**a**-tor
battery	**baterie**	ba-te-ri-ye
brakes	**brzdy**	brz-di
choke	**sytič**	si-tich
clutch	**spojka**	spoy-ka

43

engine	**motor**	mo-tor
exhaust pipe	**výfuk**	v**ee**-fook
fuse	**pojistka**	po-yist-ka
gears	**rychlosti**	rikh-los-ti
handbrake	**ruční brzda**	rooch-n**ee** brrz-da
headlights	**přední světla**	p^rzhed-n**ee** sv^yet-la
ignition	**zapalování**	za-pa-lo-va-n**ee**
indicator	**blinkr**	blin-kr
locks	**zámky**	z**a**m-ki
radiator	**chladič**	khla-dich
reverse gear	**zpátečka**	zp**a**-tech-ka
seat belts	**bezpečnostní**	b**e**z-pech-nost-n**ee**
	pásy	p**a**-si
spark plug	**svíčka**	sv**ee**ch-ka
steering	**řízení**	^rzh**ee**-ze-n**ee**
steering	**volant**	vo-lant
wheel		
tyre	**pneumatika**	pne^w-ma-ti-ka
wheel	**kolo**	ko-lo
windscreen	**přední sklo**	p^rzhed-n**ee** sklo
windscreen	**stěrač**	st^ye-rach
wiper	**předního skla**	p^rzhed-n**ee**-ho skla

Road signs

volno

spaces

obsazeno

full

multi-storey
parking

attention
changed right
of way

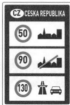

speed limits in
the Czech
Republic are in
Km/h

motorway

PRAHA Prague

Road signs

police

hospital

castle

leave town · enter town

VŠECHNY SMŮRY

all routes

POZOR!

be careful

POMALU

slow down

north

west — Západ · Sever · Východ — east

Jih

south

Staying somewhere

Hotel (booking)

••••••••••••••••••••••••••••••••••••

You can find accommodation in hotels, guesthouses, hostels and private houses. Hotels are given star ratings up to 5 stars, and in big hotels breakfast is often included in the price. Many hotels are signposted. The local tourist office will have details of accommodation in private houses, which is generally cheaper.

hotel/penzion	hotel/guesthouse
volné pokoje/obsazeno	vacancies/no vacancies
počet dětí/dospělých	number of children/adults

FACE TO FACE

A **Rád bych zamluvil jednolůžkový/
dvoulůžkový pokoj**
rad bikh si za-mlu-vil yed-no-**loo**zh-ko-vee/
dvo^w-l**oo**zh-ko-vee po-koy
I'd like to book a single/double room

B **Na kolik nocí?**
na ko-lik no-ts**ee**?
For how many nights?

A **Na tři noci**
na trzi no-tci
3 nights please

Is there a hotel here?	**Kde tu najdu hotel?** kde too nay-doo ho-tel?	
I want to book a room	**Chci si zamluvit pokoj** khtsi si zam-loo-vit po-koy	
Do you have a room	**Máte volný pokoj** m**a**-te vol-**nee** po-koy	
for tonight	**na dnes** na dnes	
for tomorrow	**na zítra** na z**ee**t-ra	
I/We want to stay...	**Chci/chceme se ubytovat na...** khtsi/khtse-me se oo-bi-to-vat na...	
How much is it per night?	**Kolik stojí jedna noc?** ko-lik sto-y**ee** yed-na nots?	

1 night	**jednu noc** yed-noo nots
2 nights	**dvě noci** dvYe no-tsi
3 nights	**tři noci** tˢrzhi no-tsi
1 week	**týden** tee-den
I want...	**Chci...** khtsi...
a single room	**pokoj pro jednu osobu** po-koy pro yed-noo o-so-boo
a double room	**pokoj pro dvě osoby** po-koy pro dvYe o-so-bi
a room for 3 people	**pokoj pro tři osoby** po-koy pro tˢrzhi o-so-bi
with bath	**s koupelnou** s koᵂ-pel-noᵂ
with shower	**se sprchou** se sprr-khoᵂ
with an extra bed for a child	**s přistýlkou pro dítě** spˢrzhi-steel-koᵂ pro dee-te
I'd like...	**Chtěl(a) bych...** khtYel(a) bikh...
a quiet room	**tichý pokoj** tYi-khee po-koy
a room on the ground floor	**pokoj v přízemí** po-koy v pˢrzhee-ze-mee

a room with a balcony	**pokoj s balkonem**
	po-koy s bal-ko-nem
Is breakfast included?	**Je v ceně zahrnuta sní daně?**
	ye v tse-n^ye za-hrr-noo-ta sn**ee**-da-n^ye?
Have you anything cheaper?	**Nemáte něco levnějšího?**
	ne-m**a**-te n^ye-tso lev-n^yey-sh**ee**-ho?
I want to see the room	**Chci si ten pokoj prohlédnout**
	khtsi si ten po-koy pro-hl**e**d-no^wt

YOU MAY HEAR...

Na kolik nocí? na ko-lik no-ts**ee**?	For how many nights?
Vaše jméno, prosím va-she ym**e**-no, pro-s**ee**m	Your name, please
Váš pas, prosím v**a**sh pas, pro-s**ee**m	Your passport, please
Máme obsazeno m**a**-me ob-sa-ze-no	We are full

Please confirm	**prosím, potvrďte**
	pro-s**ee**m, pot-vrrd^y-te
by e-mail	**e-mailem**
	ee-mey-lem
by fax	**faxem**
	fak-sem

Hotel (desk)

I've reserved...	**Rezervoval(a) jsem si...**
	re-zer-vo-val(a) ysem si...
a room	**pokoj**
	po-koy
My name is...	**Jmenuji se...**
	yme-noo-yi se...
Please can I see the room	**Mohu si prohlédnout ten pokoj**
	mo-hoo si pro-hl**e**d-no**w**t ten po-koy
I don't want this room	**Nechci tento pokoj**
	nekh-tsi ten-to po-koy
Where can I park the car?	**Kde si mohu zaparkovat auto?**
	kde si mo-hoo za-par-ko-vat a**w**-to?
What time is breakfast?	**V kolik hodin je snídaně?**
	vko-lik ho-din ye sn**ee**-da-n**Y**e?
What time is dinner?	**V kolik hodin je večeře?**
	vko-lik ho-din ye ve-che-ʳzhe?
I'd like an early morning call	**Prosil(a) bych vzbudit brzy ráno**
	pro-sil(a) bikh vzboo-dit brr-zi r**a**-no
at 6/at 7	**v šest/v sedm**
	v shest/v se-doom

51

The key, please	**Klíč, prosím**	
	kleech, pro-**seem**	
Room number...	**Číslo pokoje...**	
	chee-slo po-ko-ye...	
We will be back late	**Vrátíme se pozdě**	
	vra-**tee**-me se poz-d^ye	
Are there any messages for me?	**Nechal mi tu někdo vzkaz?**	
	ne-khal mi too n^yek-do vzkaz?	
I'm leaving tomorrow	**Zítra odjíždím**	
	zeet-ra od-yeezh-**deem**	
I'd like the bill	**Chtěl(a) bych účet**	
	kht^yel(a) bikh **oo**-chet	

Camping

●●

There are plenty of campsites and prices are
reasonable, though the facilities are often very basic.
There is usually a shop and a simple place to eat,
but not necessarily hot water or acceptable toilets.

We want to stay...	**Chceme zde zůstat...**	
	khtse-me zde z**oo**-stat...	
1 night	**jednu noc**	
	yed-noo nots	
2 nights	**dvě noci**	
	du^ye no-tsi	

3 nights	**tři noci**
	t^rzhi no-tsi
How much is it per night...?	**Kolik platíme za jednu noc...?**
	ko-lik pla-t**ee**-me za yed-noo nots...?
for a tent	**za stan**
	za stan
for a car	**za auto**
	za a^w-to
per person	**za osobu**
	za o-so-boo
Where is the nearest shop/ restaurant?	**Kde je nejbližší obchod/ restaurace?**
	kde ye ney-blizh-sh**ee** ob-khod/ res-ta^w-ra-tse?
Where is the drinking water?	**Kde je pitná voda?**
	kde ye pit-n**a** vo-da?
Is there always hot water?	**Teče pořád horká voda?**
	te-che po-^rzh**a**d hor-k**a** vo-da?

YOU MAY HEAR...

To je vaše číslo	This is your number
to ye va-she ch**ee**s-lo	
Pověste si to na stan	Fix it to your tent
po-v^yes-te si to na stan	

> **Sightseeing and tourist office** (p 68)

Self-catering

Who do we contact if there are problems?	**Když bude problém, koho máme zavolat?** kdizh boo-de pro-bl**e**m, ko-ho m**a**-me za-vo-lat?
Where is the nearest supermarket?	**Kde je nejbližší supermarket?** kde ye ney-blizh-sh**ee** soo-per-m**a**r-ket?
Where do we leave the rubbish?	**Kam máme dávat odpadky?** kam m**a**-me d**a**-vat od-pad-ki?

> **Sightseeing and tourist office** (p 68)

Shopping

Shopping phrases

....

Most large shops and department stores are open
from 9am-6pm Monday to Friday and on Saturday
mornings. In larger cities and holiday resorts there
are often shopping centres with extended opening
hours and a 24-hour hypermarket. Smaller shops
close for lunch.

FACE TO FACE

A **Co si přejete?**
   tso si p^rzhe-ye-te?
   What would you like?

B **Máte...?**
   m**a**-te...?
   Do you have...?

A **Ano. Ještě něco?**
   ano. yesh-t^ye n^ye-tso?
   Yes, we do. Anything else?

I am looking for a present for...	**Hledám dárek pro...** hle-d**a**m d**a**-rek pro...

55

Where's the nearest...?	**Kde je nejbližší...?**
	kde ye ney-blizh-shee...?
supermarket	**supermarket**
	soo-per-m**a**r-ket
baker's	**pekařství**
	pe-ka^rzh-stv**ee**
Is there a market?	**Je tu někde trh?**
	ye too n^yek-de trr-h?
Where is the market?	**Kde je trh?**
	kde ye trr-h?
How much is it?	**Kolik to stojí?**
	ko-lik to sto-y**ee**?
It is too expensive	**To je moc drahé**
	to ye mots dra-h**e**
Do you sell...?	**Prodáváte...?**
	pro-d**a**-v**a**-te...?
stamps	**známky**
	zn**a**m-ki
milk	**mléko**
	ml**e**-ko
bread	**chleba**
	khle-ba
batteries	**baterie**
	ba-te-ri-ye

YOU MAY HEAR...

| **Co si přejete?** | What would you like? |
| tso si p^rzhe-ye-te? | |

Shops

baker's	**pekařství/ pečivo**	pe-ka^rzh-stv**ee**/ pe-chi-vo
bookshop	**knihkupectví**	knih-koo-pets-tv**ee**
butcher's	**řeznictví**	^rzhez-nits-tv**ee**
clothes shop (women's)	**dámské oděvy**	d**a**m-sk**e** o-d^ye-vi
clothes shop (men's)	**pánské oděvy**	p**a**n-sk**e** o-d^ye-vi
department store	**obchodní dům**	ob-khod-n**ee** d**oo**m
greengrocer's	**ovoce a zelenina**	ovo-tse a ze-le-ni-na
grocer's	**potraviny**	pot-ra-vi-ni
hairdresser's	**kadeřnictví**	ka-de^rzh-nits-tv**ee**
optician's	**optik**	op-tik
pharmacy	**lékárna**	l**e**-k**a**r-na
shoe shop	**obuv**	o-boov
souvenir shop	**dárkové zboží**	d**a**r-ko-v**e** zbo-zh**ee**
sports shop	**sportovní zboží**	spor-tov-n**ee** zbo-zh**ee**
sweet shop	**cukrárna**	tsook-rar-na
tobacconist's	**tabák**	ta-b**a**k
toy shop	**hračky**	hrach-ki

Food (general)

biscuits	sušenky	soo-shen-ki
bread	chleba	khle-ba
bread roll	rohlík	ro-hl**ee**k
butter	máslo	m**a**s-lo
cakes	zákusky/	z**a**-koos-ki/
	koláče	ko-l**a**-che
cheese	sýr	s**ee**r
chicken	kuře	koo-^rzhe
chocolate	čokoláda	cho-ko-l**a**-da
coffee	káva	k**a**-va
cream	smetana	sme-ta-na
crisps	brambůrky	bram-b**oo**r-ki
eggs	vejce	vey-tse
fish	ryba	ri-ba
flour	mouka	mo^w-ka
ham	šunka	shoon-ka
honey	med	med
jam	džem/	dzhem/
	marmeláda	mar-me-l**a**-da
lamb	jehněčí	ye-hn^ye-ch**ee**
margarine	margarín	mar-ga-r**ee**n
milk	mléko	ml**e**-ko
oil	olej	o-ley
pasta	těstoviny	t^yes-to-vi-ni
pepper	pepř	pep^rzh

rice	rýže	ree-zhe
salt	sůl	sool
sugar	cukr	tsoo-kr
tea	čaj	chay
vinegar	ocet	o-tset
yoghurt	jogurt	yo-goort

Food (fruit and veg)

Fruit

apples	jablka	ya-bl-ka
apricots	meruňky	me-roonᵞ-ki
bananas	banány	ba-**na**-ni
cherries	třešně	tʳzhesh-nᵞe
grapefruit	grep/ grapefruit	grep/greyp-fr**oo**t
grapes	hroznové víno	hroz-no-v**e** v**ee**-no
lemons	citróny	tsi-tr**o**-ni
oranges	pomeranče	po-me-ran-che
peaches	broskve	bros-kve
pears	hrušky	hroosh-ki
plums	švestky	shvest-ki
raspberries	maliny	ma-li-ni
strawberries	jahody	ya-ho-di
watermelon	meloun	me-loʷn

aubergine	lilek	li-lek
beans	fazole	fa-zo-le
cabbage	zelí	ze-l**ee**
(white pickled)		
(green savoy)	kapusta	ka-poo-sta
carrots	mrkev	mr-kev
cauliflower	květák	kv^ye-t**ak**
celeriac	celer	tse-ler
garlic	česnek	ches-nek
leek(s)	pórek	p**o**-rek
lettuce	salát	sa-l**at**
mushrooms	houby	ho^w-bi
onions	cibule	tsi-boo-le
peas	hrášek	hr**a**-shek
peppers	papriky	pap-ri-ki
potatoes	brambory	bram-bo-ri
radishes	ředkvičky	^rzhed-kvich-ki
spinach	špenát	shpe-n**at**
tomatoes	rajčata	ray-cha-ta

60

Clothes

Look out for leather and silk goods. The word for clothes size is **velikost**, for shoe size is **číslo**.

women's sizes		men's suit sizes		shoe sizes			
UK	EU	UK	EU	UK	EU	UK	EU
10	38	36	46	2	35	7	41
12	40	38	48	3	36	8	42
14	42	40	50	4	37	9	43
16	44	42	52	5	38	10	44
18	46	44	54	6	39	11	45
20	48	46	56				

FACE TO FACE

A **Mohu si to vyzkoušet?**
mo-hoo si to viz-koᵂ-shet?
Can I try this on?

B **Ano, tudy prosím**
ano, too-di pro-seem
Certainly, this way, please

A **Máte to i v jiných barvách?**
ma-te to i vyi-neekh bar-vakh?
Do you have this in other colours?

It's for me	**Je to pro mě**
	ye to pro mnYe
It's a present	**Je to dárek**
	ye to d**a**-rek
Is it leather/silk?	**Je to kůže/hedvábí?**
	ye to k**oo**-zhe/hed-v**a**-bee?
It's too expensive	**Je to příliš drahé**
	ye to pʳzh**ee**-lish dra-h**e**
It's too big/small	**Je to příliš velké/malé**
	ye to pʳzh**ee**-lish vel-k**e**/ma-l**e**
No thanks, I don't want to buy it	**Ne děkuji, nekoupím si to**
	ne dYe-koo-yi, ne-ko**ʷ**-p**ee**m si to

YOU MAY HEAR...

Sluší vám to	It suits you
sloo-sh**ee** v**a**m to	
Jaké máte číslo bot?	What shoe size do you take?
ya-k**ee** m**a**-te ch**ee**s-lo bot?	

Shopping

Clothes (articles)

. . . .

bavlna ba-vl-na	cotton
kůže k**oo**-zhe	leather
hedvábí hed-v**a**-bee	silk
vlna vl-na	wool

> **Paying** (p 89)

belt	**pásek**	p**a**-sek
blouse	**blůza**	bl**oo**-za
bra	**podprsenka**	pod-pr-sen-ka
coat	**kabát**	ka-b**a**t
dress	**šaty**	sha-ti
hat	**klobouk**	klo-bo^wk
jacket	**bunda**	boon-da
knickers	**kalhotky**	kal-hot-ki
nightdress	**noční košile**	noch-n**ee** ko-shi-le
pyjamas	**pyžamo**	pi-zha-mo
sandals	**sandály**	san-d**a**-li
scarf (silk)	**hedvábný šátek**	hed-v**a**b-n**ee** sha-tek
scarf (wool)	**šála**	sh**a**-la
shirt	**košile**	ko-shi-le
shorts	**šortky**	short-ki
skirt	**sukně**	sook-n^Ye
socks	**ponožky**	po-nozh-ki
suit (man's)	**oblek**	ob-lek
suit (woman's)	**kostým**	kos-t**ee**m
swimsuit	**plavky**	plav-ki
tie	**kravata**	kra-va-ta
tights	**punčochové kalhoty**	poon-cho-kho-v**e** kal-ho-ti
t-shirt	**tričko**	trich-ko
track suit	**tepláková souprava**	tep-l**a**-ko-v**a** so^w-pra-va
trousers	**kalhoty**	kal-ho-ti
underpants	**slipy**	sli-pi

Maps and guides

Local tourist offices don't usually provide free
maps, but you can buy a wide selection of road
maps, street maps and guide books, often in
English. The Czech Republic has its own English-
language newspapers, and English newspapers can
be bought in large cities.

Where can I buy a map?	**Kde se kupují mapy?** kde se koo-poo-y**ee** ma-pi?
Do you have...?	**Máte...?** m**a**-te...
a road map	**autoatlas** a^w-to-at-las
a town plan	**plán města** pl**a**n mn^yes-ta
a guide book	**průvodce** pr**oo**-vod-tse
a leaflet	**brožurku** bro-zhoor-koo
in English	**v angličtině** v ang-glich-ti-n^ye
Can you show me on the map...	**Můžete mi na mapě ukázat...** m**oo**-zhe-te mi na ma-p^ye oo-k**a**-zat...

> **Asking the way** (p 24) > **Sightseeing** (p 68)

Shopping

where is...?	**kde je...?**
	kde ye...?
Please draw me a map	**Nakreslete mi, prosím, mapku**
	nak-res-le-te mi, pros**ee**m map-koo

Post office

····································

Main post offices are open Monday to Friday, and on Saturday mornings. Opening hours are generally similar to those of shops. The main post office in Prague is open 24 hours.

Do you have stamps?	**Máte známky?**
	m**a**-te zn**a**m-ki?
Stamps for postcards	**známky na pohledy**
	zn**am-kee** na po-hle-di
for letters	**na dopisy**
	na do-pi-si
to Britain	**do Británie**
	do bri-t**a**-ni-ye
to the USA	**do USA**
	do **oo**-es-**a**
to Australia	**do Austrálie**
	do a^ws-tr**a**-li-ye

> **Money** (p 88) > **Paying** (p 89)

By airmail, please	Letecky, prosím
	le-tets-ki pro-**see**m
How much is it to send this parcel?	Kolik stojí poslat tento balíček?
	ko-lik sto-y**ee** pos-lat ten-to ba-**lee**-chek?

YOU MAY HEAR...

Vyplňte to vi-pln**y**-te to	Fill this in
Tady se podepište ta-di se po-de-pish-te	Sign it here
Na poště na posh-t**y**e	At the post office

Photos

Foto-kino shops sell films, batteries and tapes for camcorders.

| I need a tape/ memory card for this camcorder | Potřebuji kazetu/ paměťovou kartu do této videokamery |
| | pot-ʳzhe-boo-yi ka-ze-too/ pa-m**y**et**y**-o-vo**w** kar-too do t**e**-to vi-de-o-ka-me-ri |

Shopping

I need a film/ memory card for this (still) camera	Potřebuji film/paměťovou kartu do tohoto fotoaparátu
	pot-ʳzhe-boo-yi film/ pa-mᵞetᵞ-o-voʷ kar-too do to-ho-to fo-to-a-pa-ra-too
a colour film	barevný film
	ba-rev-nee film
with 24/36 exposures	s dvaceti čtyřmi/třiceti šesti obrázky
	dva-tse-ti chtiʳzh-mi/trzhi-tse-ti shes-ti ob-raz-ki
When will the photos be ready?	Kdy budou fotky hotové?
	kdi bu-doʷ fot-ki ho-to-ve?
Can I take pictures here?	Mohu tady fotit?
	mo-hoo ta-di fo-tit?
Can you take a picture of us, please?	Můžete nás vyfotit, prosím?
	moo-zhe-te nas vi-fo-tit, pro-seem?

YOU MAY HEAR...

| Přejete si matné nebo lesklé? | Would you like matt or glossy prints? |
| pʳzhe-ye-te si mat-ne ne-bo les-kle? | |

67

Leisure

Sightseeing and tourist office

There are lots of tourist offices, particularly in Prague. They are generally open Monday to Friday, 9am to 6pm. Many museums, galleries and castles are closed on Mondays. Outside the tourist season, many castles and museums outside of Prague are closed or only open at weekends.

Where is the tourist office?	**Kde jsou informace pro turisty?**
	kde yso^w in-for-ma-tse pro too-ri-sti?
Is there a sightseeing tour of the city?	**Nabízíte prohlídku města?**
	na-b**ee**-z**ee**-te pro-hl**ee**d-koo mn**y**es-ta?
What can we visit in the Prague area?	**Co můžeme navštívit v okolí Prahy?**
	tso m**oo**-zhe-me nav-sht**ee**-vit vo-ko-l**ee** pra-hi?
We'd like to go to...	**Rádi bychom jeli do...**
	r**a**-di bi-khom ye-li do...

68

Are there excursions?	Pořádáte výlety?
	po-ʳzh**a**-d**a**-te v**ee**-le-ti?
How much is the guided tour?	Kolik stojí okružní jízda?
	ko-lik sto-y**ee** ok-roozh-n**ee** y**ee**z-da?
When can we visit...?	Kdy můžeme navštívit...?
	kdi m**oo**-zhe-me nav-sht**ee**-vit...?
When does it close?	Kdy zavírají?
	Kdi za-v**ee**-ra-y**ee**?
When does it leave?	Kdy se odjíždí?
	kdi se od-y**ee**zh-d**ee**?
Where from?	Odkud? od-kood?
When does it get back?	Kdy se přijede zpátky?
	kdi se pʳzhi-ye-de zp**a**t-ki?
Are there reductions for over 6os?	Mají lidé nad šedesát let slevu?
	ma-y**ee** li-d**e** nad she-de-s**a**t let sle-voo?

Entertainment

• •

Cultural guides for larger cities are available in English or on the Internet.

Where can I/we get tickets	Kde se kupují vstupenky
	kde se ku-pu-y**ee** vstu-pen-ki

> **Maps and guides** (p 64)

for tonight	**na dnes vecer**
	na dnes ve-cher
for the show	**na představení**
	na p^rzhed-sta-ve-n**ee**
for the match	**na zápas**
	na z**a**-pas
Where can we hear live music?	**Kde můžeme slyšet hudbu živě?**
	kde m**oo**-zhe-me sli-shet hood-boo zhi-v^ye?
What entertainment is there for children?	**Kam můžeme vzít děti?**
	kam m**oo**-zhe-me vz**ee**t d^ye-ti?

Leisure/interests

Many people in the Czech Republic like to spend the weekend at their **chata** (weekend cottage).

Where can we...?	**Kam můžeme...?**
	kam m**oo**-zhe-me...?
go fishing	**jít na ryby**
	y**ee**t na ri-bi
go walking	**jít se pro**
	y**ee**t se pro
play tennis	**jít hrát tenis**
	y**ee**t hr**a**t te-nis

70

hire (mountain) bikes/roller skates	**pronajmout (horská) kola/ kolečkové brusle**
	pro-nay-mo^wt (hors-k**a**) ko-la/ ko-lech-ko-v**e** brus-le
How much is it per day?	**Kolik to stojí za den?**
	ko-lik to sto-y**ee** za den?
Do you have cycling helmets?	**Půjčujete helmy pro cyklisty?**
	p**oo**y-choo-ye-te hel-mi pro tsi-kli-sti?
Is there a swimming pool here?	**Je tu koupaliště?**
	ye too ko^w-pa-lish-t**Y**e?

Music

. . . .

Local tourist offices have information about musical events and how to obtain tickets.

Are there any good concerts on?	**Hrají se nějaké dobré koncerty?**
	hra-y**ee** se n**Y**e-ya-k**e** dob-r**e** kon-tser-ti?
Where can I get tickets?	**Kde dostanu lístky?**
	kde dos-ta-noo l**ee**st-ki?
Where can we hear some...?	**Kde se hraje...?**
	kde se hra-ye...?

classical music	**vážná hudba**	
	v**a**zh –n**a** hood-ba	
jazz	**jazz**	
	dzhez	
folk songs	**lidové písničky**	
	li-do-v**e** p**ee**s-nich-ki	
I play...	**Hraji na…**	
	hra-yi na...	
the piano	**klavír**	
	kla-v**ee**r	
the guitar	**kytaru**	
	ki-ta-roo	
the clarinet	**klarinet**	
	kla-ri-ne	

YOU MAY HEAR...

Je vyprodáno	Sold out
ye vip-ro-d**a**-no	
Máme jen vstupenky k stání	We have only standing tickets
m**a**-me yen vstoo-pen-ki kst**a**-n**ee**	
Nemůžete dovnitř, už se začalo	You can't go in, it has started
ne-m**oo**-zhe-te dov-nit^rzh, oozh se za-cha-lo	

Leisure

> **Making friends** (p 20)

Cinema

• •

Some Prague cinemas provide English subtitles to
Czech films. Most foreign films are screened with
the original sound track.

What's on at the cinema?	**Co dávají v kině?**
	tso d**a**-va-y**ee** v ki-nYe?
When does (name film) start?	**Kdy začíná…?**
	kdi za-ch**ee**-na…?
How much are the tickets?	**Kolik stojí lístek?**
	ko-lik sto-y**ee** l**ee**s-tek?
Two for the (time) showing	**Dva na…**
	dva na…
Is the film in English?	**Je ten film v angličtině?**
	ye ten film vang-glich-ti-nYe?

YOU MAY HEAR…

Do sálu 1 už je vyprodáno	For screen 1 we have no tickets left
do s**a**-loo 1 oozh ye vi-pro-d**a**-no	

Theatre/opera

Non-Czech operas are mostly performed in the original language with Czech subtitles. Czech operas have English subtitles. Tickets for opera and ballet, puppet theatre and other theatres are cheap and in high demand, so make sure you buy them in advance. Smart dress is generally required when visiting traditional theatres.

What's on at the theatre?	**Co se hraje v divadle?** tso se hra-ye v di-vad-le?
How much are the tickets?	**Kolik stojí lístky?** ko-lik sto-y**ee** l**ee**st-ki?
1 ticket	**jeden lístek** ye-den l**ee**s-tek
I'd like...	**Chtěl(a) bych…** khtʸel(a) bikh…
2 tickets	**dva lístky** dvʸa l**ee**st-ki
4 tickets	**čtyři lístky** chti-ʳzhi l**ee**st-ki
for tonight	**na dnes večer** na dnes ve-cher
for tomorrow night	**na zítra večer** na z**ee**t-ra ve-cher
for 6 August	**na šestého srpna** na shes-t**e**-ho srrp-na

in the stalls	do přízemí
	do p^rzhee-ze-mee
in the circle	na balkón
	na bal-kon
in the upper circle	na druhý balkón
	na droo-hee bal-kon
How long is the interval?	Jak je dlouhá přestávka?
	yak ye dlo^w-ha p^rzhes-tav-ka?
When does the performance begin/end?	Kdy to představení začíná/končí?
	kdi to p^rzhed-sta-ve-nee za-chee-na/kon-chee?

YOU MAY HEAR...

| Nemůžete dovnitř, představení už začalo ne-**moo**-zhe-te dov-nit^rzh, p^rzhed-sta-ven**ee** uzh za-cha-lo | You can't go in, the performance has started |

Theatre/opera

75

Television

Czech terrestrial TV has 4 channels. Most foreign
films are shown dubbed.

dálkové ovládáni da**l**-ko-v**e** o-vla-da-n**ee**	remote control
populární seriál po-poo-l**ar**-n**ee** se-ri-**al**	soap
zprávy zpr**a**-vi	news
zapnout zap-no^wt	to switch on
vypnout vip-no^wt	to switch off
kreslené filmy kres-le-n**e** fil-mi	cartoons

How do I switch it on/off?	Jak se to zapíná/vypíná?	yak se to za-p**ee**-na/vi-p**ee**-na?
Please turn the volume down	Ne tak hlasitě, prosím	ne tak hla-si-t^ye, pro-s**ee**m
Please turn the volume up	Dejte to hlasitěji, prosím	dey-te to hla-si-t^ye-yi, pro-s**ee**m
What's on television?	Co se dává v televizi?	tso se d**a**-va v te-le-vi-zi?
When is the news?	Kdy jsou zprávy?	kdi yso^w zpr**a**-vi?
Are there ... any children's programmes?	Jsou na programu nějaké pořady pro děti?	yso^w na prog-ra-moo nye-ya-k**e** po-^rzha-di pro d^ye-ti?

any English-language programmes?	nějaké pořady v angličtině?
	nYe-ya-**ke** po-^rzha-di
	vang-glich-ti-nYe

YOU MAY HEAR...

| Tam jsou videokazety v angličtině | There are videotapes in English over there |
| tam yso^w vi-de-o-ka-ze-ti vang-glich-ti-nYe | |

Sport

....

Where can we...?	Kam/kde můžeme...?
	kam/kde m**oo**-zhe-me...?
go swimming	jít plavat
	y**ee**t pla-vat
go jogging	jít běhat
	y**ee**t bYe-hat
play tennis	hrát tenis
	hrat te-nis
hire rackets/ golf clubs	půjčit si tenisové rakety/ golfové hole
	p**oo**y-chit si te-ni-so-ve ra-ke-ti/ gol-fo-ve ho-le
How much is it per hour?	Kolik to stojí za hodinu?
	ko-lik to sto-y**ee** za ho-di-noo?

Sport

We'd like to see (name team) play.	Chceme se podívat jak hraje...
	khtse-me se po-d**ee**-vat yak hra-ye...
Where can we get tickets?	Kde se kupují vstupenky?
	kde se koo-poo-y**ee** vstoo-pen-ki?

YOU MAY HEAR...	
Nechcete si zahrát...?	Would you like to play...?
nekh-tse-te si za-hr**at**?...	
Je vyprodáno	Sold out
ye vi-pro-d**a**-no	

Skiing

The most popular winter sports are skiing, ice-hockey and skating. You can hire most of the equipment.

jízda na lyžích	downhill skiing
y**ee**z-da na li-zh**ee**kh	
jízda na běžkách	cross-country skiing
y**ee**z-da na bYezh-k**a**kh	
permanentka	ski pass
per-ma-nent-ka	
vlek vlek	ski lift

Leisure

I want to hire skis	**Chci si půjčit lyže**
	khtsi si p**oo**y-chit li-zhe
Does the price include...?	**Je to včetně...?**
	ye to vchet-n**Y**e...?
boots	**bot**
	bot
poles	**hůlek**
	h**oo**-lek
Can you adjust my bindings?	**Můžete mi upravit vázání?**
	m**oo**-zhe-te mi oop-ra-vit
	v**a**-z**a**-n**ee**?
How much is a pass?	**Kolik stojí permanentka?**
	ko-lik sto-y**ee** per-ma-nent-ka?
daily	**na den**
	na den
weekly	**na týden**
	na t**ee**-den

YOU MAY HEAR...

Jak dlouhé lyže chcete?	What size skis do you want?
yak dlo^w-h**e** li-zhe khtse-te?	
Jaké máte číslo bot?	What is your shoe size?
ya-k**e** m**a**-te chis-lo bot?	
Už jste někdy lyžoval?	Have you ever skied before?
oozh yste n**Y**ek-di li-zho-val?	
Chcete se učit lyžovat?	Do you want skiing lessons?
khtse-te se u-chit li-zho-vat?	

79

Walking

● ●

The Czech Republic has beautiful areas to explore with woods, lakes and mountains. Both long distance hikes and short distance walks are perfectly marked. Detailed hiking maps and guides are available in most bookshops.

Are there any guided walks?	**Pořádají se vycházky s průvodcem?**
	po-ʳzh**a**-da-yee se vi-kh**a**z-ki spr**oo**-vod-tsem?
How many kilometres is the walk?	**Kolik kilometrů je ta procházka?**
	ko-lik ki-lo-met-r**oo** ye ta pro-kh**a**z-ka?
How long will it take?	**Jak dlouho bude trvat?**
	yak dlo^w-ho boo-de trr-vat?
Is it very steep?	**Je to prudké stoupání?**
	ye to prood-k**e** sto^w-p**a**-nee?
Do we need walking boots?	**Potřebujeme pohorky?**
	pot-ʳzhe-boo-ye-me po-hor-ki?
We'd like to go climbing	**Chceme jít šplhat**
	khtse-me y**ee**t shpl-hat
Do you have a detailed map of the area?	**Máte podrobnou mapu téhle oblasti?**
	m**a**-te pod-rob-no^w ma-pu t**e**-hle ob-las-ti?

> **Maps and guides** (p 64)

Leisure

Communications

Telephone and mobile

To phone the UK from the Czech Republic, the international code is **00 44** followed by the UK area code without the leading zero. Payphones take 2, 5 and 10 Kč coins or phonecards, which can be bought at tobacconists' or newspaper kiosks. To phone the Czech Republic from the UK, the international code is **00 420**.

telefonní karta te-le-fon-**nee** kar-ta	phonecard
telefonní seznam te-le-fon-**nee** sez-nam	telephone directory
Zlaté stránky zla-**te** str**a**n-ki	yellow pages
hovor na účet volaného ho-vor na **oo**-chet vo-la-n**e**-ho	reverse-charge call
oznamovací tón o-zna-mo-va-ts**ee** ton	dialling tone
předčíslí pʳzhed-ch**ee**-sl**ee**	dialling code
mobil mo-bil	mobile, cellphone

I want to make a call	**Chci telefonovat**
	khtsi te-le-fo-no-vat
Where can I buy a phonecard?	**Kde si mohu koupit telefonní kartu?**
	kde si mo-hoo ko^w-pit te-le-fo-n**ee** kar-too?
Can you try this number for me?	**Můžete mi zavolat toto číslo?**
	m**oo**-zhe-te mi za-vo-lat to-to ch**ee**s-lo?
I can't get through	**Nemohu se dovolat**
	ne-mo-hoo se do-vo-lat
Mr/Mrs..., please	**Pana/paní... prosím**
	pa-na/pa-n**ee**... pro-s**ee**m
Extension number...	**Linka číslo...**
	lin-ka ch**ee**s-lo...
What is your mobile number?	**Jaké máte číslo mobilu?**
	ya-k**e**-m**a**-te ch**ee**s-lo mobi-lu?

FACE TO FACE

A **Haló**
ha-l**o**
Hello

B **Haló, rád(a) bych mluvil(a) s...**
ha-l**o**, r**a**d(a) bikh mloo-vil(-a) s...
Hello, I'd like to speak to ...

82

A Kdo volá?
kdo vo-**la**?
Who is calling?

B Tady (name)
ta-di...
This is ... speaking

A Okamžik/Moment
o-kam-zhik/mo-ment
Just a moment

Can I speak to...?	Mohu mluvit s...?
	mo-hoo mloo-vit s...?
This is Ian James	U telefonu Ian James
	oo te-le-fo-noo Ian James
I'll call back later	Zavolám později
	za-vo-**la**m poz-d^Ye-yi

YOU MAY HEAR...

Pokouším se vás spojit	I'm trying to connect
po-ko^w-sh**ee**m se v**a**s spo-yit	you
Je obsazeno	The line's engaged
ye ob-sa-ze-no	
Zkuste to později	Try again later
zkoos-te to poz-d^Ye-yi	
Chcete nechat vzkaz?	Do you want to leave a
khtse-te ne-khat vzkaz?	message?
To je omyl	You've got the wrong
to ye o-mil	number

Telephone and mobile

83

Po zaznění tónu zanechte vzkaz po zaz-nᵞe-nee to-noo za-nekh-te vzkaz	Please leave a message after the beep
Vypněte prosím své mobilní telefony vip-nᵞe-te pro-seem sve mo-bil-nee te-le-fo-ni	Please switch off your mobile phones

Text messaging

. . . .

I'll text you   **Pošlu ti SMS**
posh-lu ti es-em-es

Can you text me?   **Můžeš mi poslat zprávu?**
moo-zhesh mi pos-lat zpra-voo?

E-mail

. . . .

New Message	Nová zpráva
To	Komu
From	Od
Subject	Předmět
Attachment	Příloha
Send	Odeslat

Communications

Do you have e-mail?	**Máš e-mail?**
	m**a**sh **ee**-meyl?
What is your e-mail address?	**Jaká je tvoje e-mailová adresa?**
	ya-k**a** ye tvo-ye **ee**-mey-lo-v**a** a-dre-sa?
How do you spell it?	**Jak se to píše?**
	yak se to p**ee**-she?
All one word	**Jedním slovem**
	yed-n**ee**m slo-vem
All lower case	**Malá písmena**
	ma-l**a** p**ee**s-me-na
My e-mail address is...	**Moje e-mailová adresa je...**
	mo-ye **ee**-mey-lo-v**a** a-dre-sa ye...
clare.smith@ collins.co.uk	**clare tečka smith zavináč collins tečka co tečka uk**
	clare tech-ka smith za-vi-n**a**ch collins tech-ka ts**e o** tech-ka **oo** ka
Can I send an e-mail?	**Můžu si poslat e-mail?**
	m**oo**-zhoo si po-slat **ee**-meyl?
Did you get my e-mail?	**Dostal jsi můj e-mail?**
	dos-tal ysi m**oo**y **ee**-mey-l?

Internet

●●●●●●●●●●●●●●●●●●●●●●●●●●●●

Most computer and Internet terminology is in
English. The suffix for Czech Republic websites is .cz.

Is there an Internet café here?	**Je tu někde internetová kavárna?** ye too nYek-de in-ter-net-o-v**a** ka-v**a**r-na?
How much is it to log on for an hour?	**Kolik stojí hodina na síti?** ko-lik sto-y**ee** ho-di-na na s**ee**-ti?

Fax

●●●●●●●●●●●●●●●●●●●●●●●●●●●●

You can send faxes inexpensively from post offices,
bureaux and big hotels. To fax the Czech Republic
from the UK, the code is **00 420** followed by the fax
number. When faxing within the Czech Republic
you only need the fax number. To fax the UK from
the Czech Republic, the code is **00 44** followed by
the UK area code without the leading zero.

Addressing a fax

od	from
komu	to
datum	date
věc:	re:

I want to send a fax	**Chci poslat fax**	khtsi pos-lat faks
Where can I send a fax?	**Kde mohu poslat fax?**	kde mo-hoo pos-lat faks?
What is your fax number?	**Jaké je vaše číslo faxu?**	ya-ke ye va-she chees-lo fak-soo?
My fax number is...	**Číslo mého faxu je**...	chees-lo me-ho fak-soo ye...

Practicalities

Money

....

The best places to change money and travellers'
cheques are a bank (banka) or an exchange office
(směnárna). Banking hours are generally at least
8am–12pm and 1pm–4pm, Monday-Friday. Czech
and Slovak crowns are not interchangeable, so you
cannot use Czech crowns in Slovakia or vice versa.

Bankomat	cash dispenser, ATM
Kreditní karta	credit card

Where can I change money?	Kde si mohu vyměnit peníze?
	kde si mo-hoo vi-mnʸe-nit pe-n**ee**-ze?
When does the bank open/close?	Kdy se otvírá/zavírá v bance?
	kdi se ot-v**ee**-ra/za-v**ee**-ra v ban-tse?

I want to cash these travellers' cheques	Chci proplatit tyto cestovní šeky
	khtsi pro-pla-tit ti-to tses-tov-nee she-ki
Where is the nearest cash dispenser?	Kde je nejbližší bankomat?
	kde ye ney-blizh-shee ban-ko-mat?

| Váš pas, prosím | Your passport, please |
| vash pas, pro-see | |

Paying

Credit cards are now widely accepted.

účet	oo-chet	bill
stvrzenka	stvrr-zen-ka	receipt
faktura	fak-too-ra	invoice
pokladna	po-klad-na	cash desk

How much is it?	Kolik to stojí?
	ko-lik to sto-yee?
I'd like to pay	Zaplatím, prosím
	zap-la-teem, pro-seem

Paying

Where do I pay?	Kde se platí?
	kde se pla-t**ee**?
The bill, please	Účet, prosím
	oo-chet, pro-s**ee**m
I need a receipt	Potřebuji potvrzení
	pot-ʳzhe-boo-yi pot-vrr-ze-n**ee**
Is service	Je to včetně obsluhy?
included?	ye to vchet-nᵞe ob-sloo-hi?
Is VAT included?	Je to včetně DPH?
	ye to vchet-nᵞe d**e**-p**e**-h**a**?
Can I pay by	Mohu platit kreditní
credit card?	kartou?
	mo-hoo pla-tit kre-dit-n**ee**
	kar-to**ʷ**?
Do you take this	Berete tuto kreditní kartu?
credit card?	be-re-te too-to kre-dit-n**ee**
	kar-too?
Put it on my bill	Napište to na můj účet
	na-pish-te to na m**ooy** **oo**-chet

YOU MAY HEAR...	
Plaťte u pokladny	Pay at the till
platᵞ-te oo pok-lad-ni	
Nemáte drobné?	Do you have any
ne-m**a**-te drob-n**e**?	change?

> **Shopping** (p 55)

Luggage

•••

You will find left-luggage offices at railway stations,
bus stations and airports. Lockers take coins, so
make sure you have some small change on arrival.

příruční zavazadlo p^rzh**ee**-rooch-n**ee** za-va-za-dlo	hand luggage
úschovna zavazadel **oo**-skhov-na za-va-za-del	left-luggage office
skříňka na zavazadla sk^rzh**ee**nY-ka na za-va-za-dla	lockers
vozík vo-z**ee**k	trolley

My luggage . hasn't arrived	**Moje zavazadlo nedorazilo** mo-ye za-va-zad-lo ne-do-ra-zi-lo
My suitcase is damaged	**Můj kufr je rozbitý** m**oo**y koo-frr ye roz-bi-t**ee**

Repairs

•••

This is damaged. Where can I have it repaired?	**To je poškozený. Kde si to mohu nechat opravit?** to ye posh-ko-ze-ni. kde si to mo-hu ne-khat o-pra-vit?

> **Train** (p 30) > **Air travel** (p 35)   91

Can you repair	**Můžete opravit**
	M**u**-zhe-te o-pra-vit
this	**toto**
	to-to
these shoes	**tyto boty**
	ti-to bo-ti
my watch	**moje hodinky**
	mo-ye ho-din-ki

YOU MAY HEAR...

Můžete si to tu nechat do...	You can leave it here until...
m**oo**-zhe-te si to too ne-khat do...	
Bohužel, nejde to opravit	Sorry, this can't be repaired
bo-hoo-zhel, ney-de to o-pra-vit	

Laundry

Big hotels usually have a laundry service. Otherwise you can find launderettes only in large towns.

prací prášek	washing powder
pra-ts**ee** pra-shek	
pradlenka prad-len-ka	launderette
čistírna chis-t**ee**r-na	dry cleaner's

> **Breakdown** (p 42)

Practicalities

Where can I wash some clothes?	**Kde si mohu vyprat oblečení?**
	kde si mo-hoo vip-rat ob-le-che-n**ee**?
Where is the launderette?	**Kde je pradlenka?**
	kde ye prad-len-ka?
Where is the dry-cleaner's?	**Kde je čistírna?**
	kde ye chis-t**ee**r-na?

Complaints

. . . .

You need a receipt when returning goods in shops.

This doesn't work	**To nefunguje**
	to ne-foon-goo-ye
light	**světlo**
	svʸet-lo
toilet	**záchod**
	z**a**-khod
heating	**topení**
	to-pe-n**ee**
air conditioning	**klimatizace**
	kli-ma-ti-za-tse
It is dirty	**Je to špinavé**
	ye to shpi-na-ve
It is broken	**Je to rozbité**
	ye to roz-bi-t**e**

93

I want my money back	**Chci zpátky peníze**
	khtsi zp**a**t-ki pe-n**ee**-ze
I want to complain	**Chci si stěžovat**
	khtsi si st^ye-zho-vat
Please call the manager	**Zavolejte vedoucího, prosím**
	za-vo-ley-te ve-do^w-ts**ee**-ho, pro-s**ee**m
The bill is not correct	**Účet není v pořádku**
	oo-chet ne-n**ee** v po-^rzh**a**d-koo

Problems

Can you help me?	**Můžete mi pomoct?**
	m**oo**-zhe-te mi po-motst?
Is there someone here who speaks English?	**Je tu někdo, kdo mluví anglicky?**
	ye too n^yek-do, kdo mloo-v**ee** ang-glits-ki?
I'm lost	**Zabloudil(a) jsem**
	zab-lo^w-dil(a) ysem
I need to go to...	**Potřebuji se dostat...**
	pot-^rzhe-boo-yi se dos-tat...
to this address	**na tuto adresu**
	na tooto ad-re-soo
to the station	**na nádraží**
	na n**a**d-ra-zhee

94

I've missed my train	Zmeškal(a) jsem vlak
	zmesh-kal(a) ysem vlak
the connection	**spojení**
	spo-ye-n**ee**
the plane	**letadlo**
	le-tad-lo
The coach has left without me	**Autobus odejel beze mne**
	a^w-to-boos o-de-yel be-ze mne
Can you show me how this works?	**Můžete mi ukázat jak to funguje?**
	moo-zhe-te mi oo-ka-zat yak to foon-goo-ye?

Emergencies

policie	police
158 (emergency phone no.)	
požárníci	fire service
150 (emergency phone no.)	
sanitka	ambulance
155 (emergency phone no.)	
doktor	doctor

Help!	**Pomoc!**
	po-mots!
Fire!	**Hoří!**
	ho-^rzh**ee**!

95

Can you help me?	Můžete mi pomoct?
	m**oo**-zhe-te mee
	po-motst?
There's been an	Stala se nehoda
accident	sta-la se ne-ho-da
Please call the	Zavolejte policii, prosím
police	za-vo-ley-te po-li-tsi-yi, pro-s**ee**m
an ambulance	sanitku
	sa-nit-koo
Someone has	Někdo byl zraněn/poražen
been injured/	autem
knocked down	nʸek-do bil zra-nʸen/po-ra-zhen
by a car	aoo-tem
Where is the	Kde je policejní stanice?
police station?	kde ye po-li-tsey-n**ee** sta-ni-tse?
I've been robbed/	Byl(a) jsem okraden(a)/
attacked/raped	napaden(a)/znásilněna
	bil(a) ysem ok-ra-den(a)/
	na-pa-den(a)/zn**a**-sil·nʸe-na
I want to speak	Chci mluvit se policistkou
to a female	khtsi mloo-vit se po-li-tsist-koᵂ
police officer	
Someone has	Někdo mi ukradl...
stolen...	nʸek-do mi oo-kra-dl...
I've lost...	Ztratil(a) jsem...
	ztra-til(a) ysem...
my camera	fotoaparát
	fo-to-a-pa-r**a**t

96

my passport	**pas**
	pas
my money	**peníze**
	pe-n**ee**-ze
my air ticket	**letenku**
	le-ten-koo
My car has been stolen	**Ukradli mi auto**
	oo-krad-li mi a^w-to
My car has been broken into	**Někdo se mi vloupal do auta**
	n^Yek-do se mi vlo^w-pal do a^w-ta
I need to make a phone call	**Musím si zavolat**
	moo-s**ee**m si za-vo-lat
I need a report for my insurance	**Potřebuji hlášení kvůli pojištění**
	pot-ʳzhe-boo-yi hl**a**-she-n**ee** kv**oo**-li po-yish-t^Ye-n**ee**
Please call the British Embassy	**Zavolejte, prosím, britské velvyslanectví**
	za-vo-ley-te, pro-s**ee**m, brit-sk**e** vel-vis-la-nets-tv**ee**
How much is the fine?	**Kolik dělá ta pokuta?**
	ko-lik d^Ye-l**a** ta po-koo-ta?
Where do I pay it?	**Kde ji mam zaplatit?**
	kde yi mam zap-la-tit?
I'm sorry	**Omlouvám se**
	om-lo^w-v**a**m se

Health

Pharmacy

•••

Opening hours are the same as most other shops.
Large pharmacies do not close for lunch.

Where is the nearest pharmacy?	**Kde je nejbližší lékárna?** kde ye ney-blizh-sh**ee** le-k**a**r-na?
Can you give me something for...	**Potřebuji něco proti...** pot-ʳzhe-boo-yi n^ye-tso pro-ti...
a headache	**bolesti hlavy** bo-les-ti hla-vi
diarrhoea	**průjmu** pr**oo**y-moo
car sickness	**nevolnosti v autě** ne-vol-nos-ti va^w-t^ye
Is it safe for...?	**Je to bezpečné pro...?** ye to bez-pech-n**e** pro...?
babies	**nemluvňata** nem-loov-n^ya-ta

children	**děti**
	dYe-ti
pregnant women	**těhotné ženy**
	tYe-hot-ne zhe-ni
What is the dose?	**Jaké je dávkování?**
	ya-ke ye dav-ko-va-nee?

YOU MAY HEAR...

Třikrát denně	Three times a day
t^rzhi-kr**a**t de-n^Ye	
před jídlem/s jídlem/ po jídle	before/with/after/ meals
p^rzhed y**ee**d-lem/s y**ee**d-lem/ po y**ee**d-le	

FACE TO FACE

A **Necítím se dobře**
ne-ts**ee**-t**ee**m se –dob-^rzhe
I don't feel well

B **Máte teplotu?**
m**a**-te tep-lo-too?
Do you have a temperature?

A **Ne, ale bolí mě tady...**
ne, ale bo-l**ee** mn^Ye ta-di...
No, but I have a pain here

Pharmacy

Doctor

. . . .

The Yellow Pages lists doctors' addresses (with the title **MUDr** before the name). Many doctors speak some English and in cases of emergency will refer you to a hospital. If you do not have an EU health card, you will usually be required to pay for treatment in cash.

nemocnice ne-mots-ni-tse	hospital
oddělení úrazů od-dYe-le-nee oo-ra-zoo	casualty department
předpis pᵣzhed-pis	prescription
objednání k lékaři ob-yed-na-nee kle-ka-ᵣzhi	appointment
poliklinika/středisko po-lik-li-ni-ka/stᵣzhe-dis-ko	local health centre

I need a doctor	**Potřebuji lékaře**	
	pot-ᵣzhe-boo-yi le-ka-ᵣzhe	
I have a pain here	**Bolí mě tady**	
	bo-lee mnYe ta-di	
My son is ill	**Můj syn je nemocný**	
	mooy sin ye ne-mots-nee	
My daughter is ill	**Moje dcera je nemocná**	
	mo-ye dtse-ra ye ne-mots-na	

Health

I'm pregnant	**Jsem těhotná**
	ysem t^ye-hot-n**a**
I'm diabetic	**Jsem diabetik**
	ysem di-ya-be-tik
(male and female)	**Mám cukrovku**
	m**a**m tsoo-krov-koo
I need a tetanus injection	**Potřebuji protitetanovou injekci**
	pot-^rzhe-boo-yi pro-ti-te-ta-no-vo^w in-yek-tsi
I'm allergic to penicillin	**Jsem alergický(á) na penicilín**
	ysem a-ler-gits-k**ee(a)** na pe-ni-tsi-l**ee**n
I'm on the pill	**Beru antikoncepci**
	be-roo an-ti-kon-tsep-tsi
I have high blood pressure	**Mám vysoký krevní tlak**
	m**a**m vi-so-k**ee** krev-n**ee** tlak
Here are the drugs I'm taking	**Tady jsou léky, které beru**
	ta-di yso^w l**e**-ki, kte-r**e** be-roo
Will I have to pay?	**Budu muset platit?**
	boo-doo moo-set pla-tit?
How much will it cost?	**Kolik to bude stát?**
	ko-l**i**k to boo-de st**a**t?
Can you give me the receipt for the insurance?	**Můžete mi dát potvrzení pro pojišťovnu?**
	m**oo**-zhe-te mi d**a**t pot-vrr-ze-n**ee** pro po-yish-t^yov-noo?

Není to vážné	It is not serious
ne-n**ee** to v**a**zh-n**e**	
Budete muset do nemocnice	You will have to go to hospital
bu-de-te moo-set do ne-mots-ni-tse	

Dentist

•••••••••••••••••••••••••••••••••••••••

Dentists are listed in the Yellow Pages (with the title **MUDr** before the name). Payment is usually made in cash.

I need a dentist	**Potřebuji zubaře**
	pot-ᶠzhe-boo-yi zoo-ba-ᶠzhe
He/She has toothache	**Bolí ho/ji zub**
	bo-l**ee** ho/yi zoob
This hurts	**To bolí**
	to bo-l**ee**
Can you give me something for the pain?	**Můžete mi dát něco proti bolesti?**
	m**oo**-zhe-te mee d**a**t ne-tso pro-tee bo-les-tee?

> **Emergencies** (p 95)

Health

Can you repair my dentures?	**Můžete mi opravit zubní protézy?**
	m**oo**-zhe-te mi op-ra-vit zoob-n**ee** pro-t**e**-zi?
Do I have to pay?	**Musím platit?**
	moo-s**ee**m pla-tit?
How much will it be?	**Kolik to bude stát?**
	ko-lik to boo-de st**a**t?
I need a receipt for my insurance	**Potřebuji potvrzení pro svou pojišťovnu**
	pot-ʳzhe-boo-yi pot-vrr-ze-n**ee** o zap-la-tse-n**ee** pro svo**ʷ** po-yish-tʸov-noo

YOU MAY HEAR...

Musím ten zub vytrhnout	I'll have to take it out
moo-s**ee**m ten zoob vi-trr-hno**ʷ**t	
Potřebujete plombu	You need a filling
pot-ʳzhe-boo-ye-te plom-boo	
To asi bude trochu bolet	This might hurt a little
to-asi boo-de tro-khoo bo-let	

Dentist

> **Pharmacy** (p 98)   103

Different types of travellers

Disabled travellers

••

The approach to disabled people has changed in
recent years. However, there are still few facilities,
except in newly-built or recently renovated hotels
which cater for the disabled.

Are there facilities for the disabled?	**Je tu vybavení pro zdravotně postižené?** ye too vi-ba-ve-n**ee** pro zdra-vot-n^ye pos-ti-zhe-n**e**?
Is there a toilet for the disabled?	**Je tu záchod pro zdravotně postižené?** ye too z**a**-khod pro zdra-vot-n^ye pos-ti-zhe-n**e**?
Do you have any bedrooms on the ground floor?	**Máte ložnice v přízemí?** ma-te lozh-ni-tse v p^rzh**ee**-ze-m**ee**?
Can you visit ... in a wheelchair?	**Mohou vozíčkáři do...** mo-ho^w vo-z**ee**ch-k**a**-^rzhi do...

Is there a lift?	**Je tu výtah?**
	ye too v**ee**-ta-h?
Where is the lift?	**Kde je výtah?**
	kde ye v**ee**-ta-h?
Do you have	**Máte k dispozici vozíčky?**
wheelchairs?	m**a**-te k dis-po-zi-tsi vo-z**ee**ch-ki?
Is there a	**Dáváte slevu pro**
reduction for	**postižené?**
disabled people?	da-v**a**-te sle-voo pro pos-ti-zhe-n**e**?
Is there	**Mohu si někde sednout?**
somewhere I	mo-hoo si nᵞek-de sed-no^wt?
can sit down?	

With kids

••

Public transport is free for children under 6.
Children under 15 pay a reduced fare.

A child's ticket	**Dětský lístek**
	dᵞet-sk**ee** l**ee**s-tek
He/She is...	**je mu/jí... let**
years old	ye moo/y**ee**... let
Is there a	**Mají děti slevu?**
reduction for	ma-y**ee** dᵞe-ti sle-voo?
children?	

> **Pharmacy** (p 98) > **Doctor** (p 100)

Do you have a children's menu?	**Máte dětská jídla?**
	m**a**-te d**Y**et-sk**a** y**ee**d-la?
Is it OK to take children?	**Můžeme vzít s sebou děti?**
	m**oo**-zhe-me vz**ee**t s se-bo**w** d**Y**e-ti?
Do you have...?	**Máte...?**
	m**a**-te...?
a high chair	**dětskou židli?**
	d**Y**et-sko**w** zhid-li
a cot	**dětskou postýlku**
	d**Y**et-sko**w** po-st**ee**l-koo
Do you have any children?	**Máte děti?**
	m**a**-te d**Y**e-ti?
I have two children	**Mám dvě děti**
	m**a**m dv**Y**e d**Y**e-ti
He/She is 10 years old	**Je mu/jí deset let**
	ye moo/y**ee** de-set let

Reference

Alphabet

This is the alphabet for dictionary purposes. NB **ch** follows **h**.

Letter	Symbol	Sounds like
A a	a	**fat**
B b	b	**balloon**
C c	ts	**bits**
Č č	ch	**church**
D d	d	**dad**
E e	e	**pet**
F f	f	**fur**
G g	g	**get**
H h	h	**home**
CH ch	kh	**loch** (Scottish pronunciation)
I i	i	**pill**
J j	y	**yes**
K k	k	**kite**
L l	l	**late**

M	m	m	mi**lk**
N	n	n	**no**
O	o	o	**po**p
P	p	p	p**eace**
R	r	r, rr	**red** (rolled)
Ř	ř	ʳzh	(combined 'r' and 'zh')
S	s	s	**so**n
Š	š	sh	**sh**ut
T	t	t	**to**p
U	u	oo	**boo**k
V	v	v	**ve**t
W	w	v	**ve**t
X	x	x	fa**x**
Y	y	y	p**ill**
Z	z	z	**ze**bra
Ž	ž	zh	plea**s**ure

Spell it please	**Hláskujte, prosím**
	hla**s**-kooy-te, pro-s**ee**m
B for balloon	**B jako balon**
	b ya-ko ba-lon

Measurements and quantities

....

Czechs usually buy their shopping in decagrams
(=10 grams).

1lb is approx. 0.5 kilo 1 pint is approx. 0.5 litre

Liquids

½ litre of...	**půl litru...**
	pool lit-roo...
a litre of...	**jeden litr...**
	ye-den li-trr...
½ bottle of...	**půl lahve...**
	pool la-hve...
a bottle of...	**láhev...**
	la-hev...
a glass of...	**sklenice...**
	skle-ni-tse...

Weights

100 grams	**deset deka (10 dkg)**
	de-set de-ka
half a kilo of...	**půl kila...**
	pool ki-la...
a kilo of...	**jedno kilo...**
	yed-no ki-lo...

Food

a slice of...	**plátek...**
	pla-tek...
a portion of...	**porce...**
	por-tse...
a box of...	**krabice...**
	kra-bi-tse...
a packet of...	**krabička...**
	kra-bich-ka...
a tin of...	**plechovka...**
	ple-khov-ka...
a jar of...	**sklenice...**
	skle-ni-tse...

Miscellaneous

...crowns worth of...	**...za ... korun (Kč)**
	...za ... ko-roon
a quarter	**jedna čtvrtina**
	yed-na chtvr-ti-na
ten per cent	**deset procent**
	de-set prot-sent
more than	**více než**
	vee-tse nezh
less than	**méně než**
	me-nYe nezh

double	**dvojitý**
	dvo-yi-t**ee**
twice	**dvakrát**
	dva-kr**a**t

Numbers

• •

0	**nula** noo-la
1	**jeden** (m)/**jedna** (f)/**jedno** (nt)
	yed-en/yed-na/yed-no
2	**dva** (m)/**dvě** (f/nt) dva/dvʸe
3	**tři** t^rzhi
4	**čtyři** chti-^rzhi
5	**pět** pʸet
6	**šest** shest
7	**sedm** se-doom
8	**osm** o-soom
9	**devět** de-vʸet
10	**deset** de-set
11	**jedenáct** ye-de-n**a**tst
12	**dvanáct** dva-n**a**tst
13	**třináct** t^rzhi-n**a**tst
14	**čtrnáct** chtrr-n**a**tst
15	**patnáct** pat-n**a**tst
16	**šestnáct** shest-n**a**tst

17	**sedmnáct** se-doom-n**a**tst
18	**osmnáct** o-soom-n**a**tst
19	**devatenáct** de-va-te-n**a**tst
20	**dvacet** dva-tset
21	**dvacet jedna** dva-tset yed-na
22	**dvacet dva** dva-tset dva
23	**dvacet tři** dva-tset t^rzhi
24	**dvacet čtyři** dva-tset chti-^rzhi
25	**dvacet pět** dva-tset p^yet
30	**třicet** t^rzhi-tset
40	**čtyřicet** chti-^rzhi-tset
50	**padesát** pa-de-s**a**t
60	**šedesát** she-de-s**a**t
70	**sedmdesát** se-doom-de-s**a**t
80	**osmdesát** o-soom-de-s**a**t
90	**devadesát** de-va-de-s**a**t
100	**sto** sto
110	**sto deset** sto de-set
500	**pět set** p^yet set
1,000	**tisíc** ti-s**ee**ts
2,000	**dva tisíce** dva ti-s**ee**t-se
1 million	**milión** mi-li-y**o**n

1st	**první** prrv-n**ee**	6th	**šestý** shes-t**ee**
2nd	**druhý** droo-h**ee**	7th	**sedmý** sed-m**ee**
3rd	**třetí** tʳzhe-ti	8th	**osmý** os-m**ee**
4th	**čtvrtý** chtvrr-t**ee**	9th	**devátý** de-v**a**-tee
5th	**pátý** p**a**-tee	10th	**desátý** de-s**a**-tee

Days and months

●●●●●●●●●●●●●●●●●●●●●●●●●●●●●●●●●●●●●●●

Days

Monday	**pondělí**	pon-dʸe-l**ee**
Tuesday	**úterý**	**oo**-te-r**ee**
Wednesday	**středa**	stʳzhe-da
Thursday	**čtvrtek**	chtvrr-tek
Friday	**pátek**	p**a**-tek
Saturday	**sobota**	so-bo-ta
Sunday	**neděle**	ne-dʸe-le

Months

January	**leden**	le-den
February	**únor**	**oo**-nor
March	**březen**	bᶠzhe-zen
April	**duben**	doo-ben
May	**květen**	kvῨe-ten
June	**červen**	cher-ven
July	**červenec**	cher-ve-nets
August	**srpen**	sr-pen
September	**září**	za-ᶠzh**ee**
October	**říjen**	ᶠzh**ee**-yen
November	**listopad**	li-sto-pad
December	**prosinec**	pro-si-nets

Seasons

spring	**jaro**	ya-ro
summer	**léto**	l**e**-to
autumn	**podzim**	pod-zim
winter	**zima**	zi-ma

What's the date today?	**Kolikátého je dnes?**
	ko-li-k**a**-t**e**-ho ye dnes?
It's the 10th of March	**Je desátého března**
	ye de-s**a**-t**e**-ho bᶠzhez-na
on Saturday	**v sobotu**
	v so-bo-too

every Saturday	**každou sobotu**	
	kazh-do^w so-bo-too	
next Saturday	**příští sobotu**	
	p^rzh**ee**sh-t**ee** so-bo-too	
last Saturday	**minulou sobotu**	
	mi-noo-lo^w so-bo-too	
this Saturday	**tuto sobotu**	
	too-to so-bo-too	
in June	**v červnu**	
	v cherv-noo	
at the beginning of June	**na začátku června**	
	na za-ch**a**t-koo erv-na	
at the end of June	**na konci června**	
	na kon-tsi cherv-na	
before summer	**před létem**	
	p^rzhed l**e**-tem	
during the summer	**během léta**	
	b^ye-hem l**e**-ta	
after the summer	**po létě**	
	po l**e**-t^ye	

Time

•••••••••••••••••••••••••••••••••••••

The 24-hour clock is used in the Czech Republic.
Note that Czechs say 'half to' and 'three quarters
to' the next hour, rather than 'half past' or 'quarter
past' the preceding hour.

quarter (13.15)	**čtvrt na dvě**
	chtvrrt na dvYe
half (13.30)	**půl druhé**
	p**oo**l droo-h**e**
three quarters (13.45)	**tři čtvrtě na dvě**
	t^rzhi chtvrr-tYe na dvYe
What time is it?	**Kolik je hodin?**
	ko-lik ye ho-din?
It's...	**Je...**
	ye...
it's midday	**je poledne**
	ye po-led-ne
it's midnight	**je půlnoc**
	ye p**oo**l-nots
it's 1 o'clock	**je jedna hodina**
	ye yed-na ho-di-na
it's 9 o'clock	**je devět hodin**
	ye de-vYet ho-din
9	**devět hodin**
	de-vYet ho-din

9.10	**devět hodin deset minut**
	de-vyet ho-dín de-set mi-noot
9.15	**devět hodin patnáct minut**
	de-vyet ho-dín pat-natst mi-noot
a quarter past 9	**čtvrt na deset**
	chtvrrt na de-set
9.30	**devět hodin třicet minut**
	de-vyet ho-dín tʳzhi-tset mi-noot
half past 9	**půl desáté**
	pool de-sa-te
9.45	**devět hodin čtyřicet pět minut**
	de-vyet ho-dín chti-ʳzhi-tset pyet mi-noot
a quarter to 10	**tři čtvrtě na deset**
	tʳzhi chtvrr-tye na de-set
9.50	**devět hodin padesát minut**
	de-vyet ho-dín pa-de-sat mi-noot
10 to 10	**za deset minut deset**
	za de-set mi-noot de-set

| **Bohužel nevím** | Sorry, I don't know |
| bo-hoo-zhel ne-veem | |

Time

Time phrases

●●●●●●●●●●●●●●●●●●●●●●●●●●●●●●●●●●●●

When does ... open?	**Kdy otevírá...?** kdi o-te-**vee**-r**a**...?
When does ... close?	**Kdy zavírá...?** kdi za-**vee**-ra...?
When does ... begin?	**Kdy začíná...?** kdi za-ch**ee**-na...?
When does ... finish?	**Kdy končí...?** kdi kon-ch**ee**...?
at 3 o'clock	**ve 3 hodiny** ve trzi ho-di-ni
before 3 o'clock	**před třetí hodinou** p^rzhed t^rzhe-t**ee** ho-di-no^w
after 3 o'clock	**po třetí hodině** po t^rzhe-t**ee** ho-di-n^ye
today	**dnes** dnes
tonight	**dnes večer** dnes ve-cher
tomorrow	**zítra** z**ee**-tra
yesterday	**včera** vche-ra

Eating out

Eating places

••••••••••••••••••••••••••••••

For many Czech families the main meal of the day is lunch (**oběd**), usually hot. Breakfast (**snídaně**) and dinner (**večeře**) are often cold. At weekends lunch is more elaborate, always including soup, a main course and dessert. Traditionally, Czech food is meat-based, though this is rapidly changing (see VEGETARIAN). There are plenty of places serving foreign dishes, too.

bufet Self-service snack bar serving simple hot and cold snacks, often eaten standing up.

kavárna Café serving coffee, cakes, various refreshments, alcoholic and non-alcoholic drinks.

PIVNICE Type of pub selling mostly beer.

hospoda/hostinec/pohostinství Typical Czech pub with basic, traditional Czech dishes.

cukrárna Sweet shop (patisserie) serving cakes,
ice cream, soft drinks, coffee and tea; some
function as cafés, others are just take-aways.

restaurace Restaurant serving set-price meals,
à la carte menu and drinks.

vinárna Restaurant serving a set-price menu and
à la carte menu with a wide range of wines.

In a bar/café

People normally drink coffee, soft drinks, mineral
water or beer during the day and with meals. If you
want to drink beer, go to a **hospoda** or **pivnice**
(types of pub), for wine try a **vinárna** and for coffee
a **kavárna**. Places serving tea, **čajovny**, have
become popular recently.

FACE TO FACE

A **Co si dáte?**
tso si d**a**-te?
What will you have?

B **Dvě piva, prosím**
dv^ye pi-va, pro-s**ee**m
Two beers, please

a tea	**čaj**	
	chay	
a beer	**pivo**	
	pi-vo	
2 teas	**dva čaje**	
	dva cha-ye	
a coffee	**kávu**	
	k**a**-voo	
please	**prosím**	
	pro-s**ee**m	
a white coffee	**kávu s mlékem**	
	k**a**-voo sml**e**-kem	
a black coffee	**černou kávu**	
	cher-no^w k**a**-voo	
with milk	**s mlékem**	
	s ml**e**-kem	
with/without sugar	**s cukrem/bez cukru**	
	s tsook-rem/bez tsook-roo	
with lemon	**s citrónem**	
	s tsi-tr**o**-nem	
with ice	**s ledem**	
	le-dem	
a bottle of mineral water	**láhev minerálky**	
	l**a**-hev mi-ne-r**a**l-ki	
sparkling	**perlivou**	
	per-li-vou	
still	**neperlivou**	
	ne-per-li-vou	

for two	**pro dva**
	pro dva
for me	**pro mě**
	pro mnYe
for him	**pro něho**
	pro nYe-ho
for her	**pro ni**
	pro ni
for us	**pro nás**
	pro nas

In a restaurant

In Czech restaurants, service is not usually included in the bill. It is customary to tip.

FACE TO FACE

A Rád(a) bych si zamluvil(a) stůl pro... lidí na dnes večer

r**a**d(-a) bikh si zam-loo-vil(-a) st**oo**l pro... li-d**ee** na dnes ve-cher

I'd like to book a table for ... for tonight

B Ano. V kolik hodin?

ano. v ko-lik ho-din?

Yes, for what time?

The menu, please	**Jídelní lístek, prosím**
	yee-del-nee lees-tek, pro-seem
Is there a dish of the day?	**Máte denní menu?**
	ma-te den-nee me-noo?
Can you tell me what this is?	**Můžete mi říct co to je?**
	moo-zhe-te mi ʳzheetst tso to ye?
I'll have this	**Chtěl(a) bych toto**
	khtʸel(a) bikh to-to
Excuse me!	**Promiňte!**
	pro-minʸ-te!
Could we have some	**Přineste prosím...**
	pʳzhi-nes-te pro-seem...
more bread/water	**ještě chleba/vodu**
	yesh-tʸe khle-ba/vo-doo
The bill, please	**Účet, prosím**
	oo-chet, pro-seem
Where are the toilets, please?	**Kde jsou záchody, prosím?**
	kde ysou za-kho-di, pro-seem?

Vegetarian

•••••••••••••••••••••••••••••••••••••••

The Czech diet is very meat-based, but fish, pasta, omelettes and cheese dishes (the most popular being fried cheese, smažený sýr) are usually available.

Is there a vegetarian restaurant here?	**Je tady někde vegetariánská restaurace? restaurace?** ye ta-di nYek-de ve-ge-ta-ri-yan-ska res-taW-ra-tse?
Which dishes have no meat?	**Která jídla jsou bez masa?** kte-ra yid-la ysoW bez ma-sa?
Which dishes do you recommend?	**Co mi doporučíte?** tso mi do-po-roo-chee-te?
Do you have any vegetarian dishes?	**Máte nějaká vegetariánská jídla?** ma-te nYe-ya-ka ve-ge-ta-ri-yan-ska yeed-la?
What fish dishes do you have?	**Jaká rybí jídla máte?** ya-ka ri-bee yeed-la ma-te?

Vegetarian dishes

vegetariánská jídla ve-ge-ta-ri-y**a**n-sk**a** y**ee**d-la
bramborák potato pancake
čočka s vejcem lentils with egg
knedlík s vejci czech bread dumplings with eggs
lečo s vejcem spicy vegetable dish with eggs
míchaná vejce scrambled eggs
omeleta se špenátem spinach omelette
omeleta se žampiony mushroom omelette
smažený Hermelín fried Camembert-style cheese
smažený sýr fried cheese
sýrová mísa cheese platter
zeleninové karbanátky vegetable burgers
zeleninové rizoto vegetable risotto

Beers, wines and spirits

Czech beer is of outstanding quality and very cheap.
Beers are graded by degrees, according to their
original malt content:

desítka de-s**eet**-ka (10)
dvanáctka dva-n**a**tst-ka (12).

Most Czech beers are light, lager-style beers,
světlé (sv**y**et-l**e**). Dark beers, **tmavé** (tma-v**e**),
are usually sweeter. The most common beers are:

Pilsner Urquell (Plzeňský prazdroj),
Gambrinus, Staropramen, Budvar (Budweiser),
Radegast, Velkopopovický kozel, Starobrno,
Bernard and Krušovice.

Pubs serve beer in half-litre mugs. A tally is kept on
a slip of paper at your table and you pay at the end
of the evening. Beer bought in a shop includes a
deposit for the bottle.

While Bohemia is mainly a beer country,
Moravia, particularly the southern part, produces
wine (as does Slovakia). Visits to Moravian wine-
cellars are popular, not only for the wine but also
for the wonderful music and singing.

The best known spirits are becherovka (a digestive
herb liqueur) and slivovice (plum brandy). Herb
liqueurs are worth mentioning are the famous
Becherovka, Borovička (made with juniper
berries), Praděd and Fernet (with its distinctive
bitter taste).

The local rum, tuzemák, has a different flavour
from other better-known rums. In winter, it forms
the basis of the popular hot drink grog. Absinth
has also enjoyed a resurgence in recent years.

I'd like a beer	**Chtěl(a) bych pivo**
	khtYel(-a) bikh pi-vo
Can you	**Můžete nám doporučit**
recommend a	**nějaké dobré víno?**
good wine?	m**oo**-zhe-te n**a**m do-po-roo-chit
	nYe-ya-k**e** dob-r**e** v**ee**-no?
A bottle.../	**Láhev.../Skleničku...**
A glass...	l**a**-hev.../skle-nich-koo...
of beer/of wine	**piva/vína**
	pi-va/v**ee**-na
of red wine	**červeného vína**
	cher-ve-n**e**-ho v**ee**-na
of white wine	**bílého vína**
	b**ee**-l**e**-ho v**ee**-na
of dry white wine	**suchého bílého vína**
	soo-kh**e**-ho b**ee**-le-ho v**ee**-na
of sparkling wine	**sektu**
	sek-too
of spritzer	**střiku**
	st^rzhi-koo
mulled wine	**svařené víno**
	sva-^rzhe-n**e** v**ee**-no
The wine list,	**Vinný lístek, prosím**
please	vi-n**ee** l**ee**s-tek, pro-s**ee**m
What spirits do	**Jaké máte lihoviny?**
you have?	ya-k**e** m**a**-te li-ho-vi-ni?

Menu reader

alkoholické nápoje alcoholic beverages
americké brambory roast potato wedges with skins
ananas pineapple
anglická slanina bacon
angrešt gooseberry
artyčoky artichokes

bábovka traditional marble cake
banán banana
bažant pheasant
Becherovka digestive, herb liquer
bezmasá jídla vegetarian food
biftek se šunkou a vejci minute steak with ham and egg
bílá káva white coffee
bílá klobása white sausage (veal and pork with herbs)
bílé víno white wine
bílé zelí white cabbage
bílý chléb white bread
blatenské zlato slightly sharp, semi-soft yellow cheese

bobkový list bay leaf

boršč borsch

borůvky blueberries

bramborák potato pancake

bramborová kaše potato purée/mashed
 potatoes

bramborová placka potato pancake

bramborová polévka potato soup

bramborové knedlíky potato dumplings

bramborové knedlíky plněné uzeným
 masem s cibulkou potato dumplings filled with
 smoked meat with onions

bramborové krokety potato croquettes

bramborové šišky small flour and potato
 dumplings served with sweet coating

bramborový salát potato salad

brambory potatoes

brambůrky crisps

broskev peach

brusinky cranberries

bryndza sheep's milk cheese

bryndzové halušky gnocchi (small dumplings)
 with sheep's milk cheese and diced bacon

bublanina sponge with fruit

buchty buns/yeast dumpling filled with various
 jams or cottage cheese

buchty s povidly buns filled with thick plum jam

buchty s tvarohem buns filled with cottage
 cheese

buchty s mákem buns filled with poppy seeds
bujón broth with egg
buráky/burské oříšky peanuts
burčák m alcoholic wine must (very young, frothy, yeasty wine)
buřty s cibulí sausages with onions
bylinkový čaj herbal tea
bylinky herbs

celer celeriac
celozrnný wholemeal
celozrnný chléb wholemeal bread
cibulová polévka onion soup
cibule onion
cibulový koláč onion flan
cikánská pečeně Gypsy-style roast
citron lemon
cuketa courgette
cukr sugar
cukroví cookies, biscuits, sweets
čaj tea
čaj s citronem tea with lemon
čaj s mlékem tea with milk
čaj s rumem tea with rum
čedar cheddar cheese
černá káva black coffee
černé pivo dark beer
černý čaj black tea
černý chléb rye bread

černý rybíz blackcurrant
čerstvé ovoce fresh fruit
červená řepa beetroot
červené víno red wine
červené zelí red cabbage
červený rybíz redcurrant
česnek garlic
česneková polévka garlic soup
česneková pomazánka garlic spread
čevapčiči meatballs
čočka lentils
čočka na kyselo savoury lentils
čočková polévka lentil soup
čočkový salát lentil salad
čokoláda chocolate
čokoládová zmrzlina chocolate ice-cream
čokoládový dort chocolate cake/gateau

ďábelské toasty spicy toasts
dalamánek dark bread roll
dary moře seafood
datle dates
debrecínská pečeně Hungarian-style ham
  (with spicy crust)
denní menu dish of the day
dětská jídla/porce children's meals/portions
domácí home-made
dort cake
dršťková polévka tripe soup

drůbež poultry
dušené zelí stewed cabbage
dušený, dušená, dušené steamed, stewed
dva, tři, čtyři kopečky (of ice cream) two, three, four scoops
dýně pumpkin, vegetable marrow
džem jam
džus juice

eidam edam cheese
ementál Swiss-style cheese

fazole beans
fazolová polévka bean soup
fazolový salát bean salad
fíky figs
flambovaný(-á/-é) flambéed
fondue cheese fondue

grapefruit, grep grapefruit
grilovaný(-á/-é) grilled
grog hot rum and water
guláš goulash (stewed diced beef and pork with paprika served usually with dumplings)
guláš ze zvěřiny game goulash
gulášová polévka goulash soup
gyros kebab

hamburger hamburger
halušky gnocchi served with bacon and sheep cheese
Herkules hard spicy salami
Hermelín camembert-style cheese
heřmánkový čaj camomile tea
hlávkový salát lettuce
hlavní chod main course
horký(-á/-é) hot, warm
horká čokoláda hot chocolate
hořčice mustard
hořká čokoláda dark, bitter chocolate
hotová jídla ready-made dishes
houbová polévka mushroom soup
houby mushrooms
houska roll, bun
houskový knedlík Czech bread dumpling
hovězí beef
hovězí guláš beef goulash
hovězí pečeně roast beef
hovězí plátek sliced beef
hovězí polévka beef soup
hovězí vývar beef consommé
hovězí vývar s játrovými knedlíčky beef consommé with liver dumplings
hrách peas
hrachová polévka pea soup
hranolky chips, French fries
hrášek green peas

hrozinky raisins
hroznové víno grapes
hruška pear
hruškovice pear brandy
hřebíček cloves
humr lobster
husa goose
husí játra goose liver

chleba bread
chlebíčky small open sandwiches
chlupaté knedlíky se zelím potato dumplings
  with cabbage made from raw grated potato, flour
  and egg
chod course
chodský koláč large lattice pie from south
  western Bohemia, with cottage cheese, plum jam
  and poppy seed filling
chřest asparagus
chřestový krém cream of asparagus soup
chuťovky savouries

jablečný/jablkový závin/štrůdl apple
  pastry/strudel
jablko apple
jahody strawberries
jarní míchaný salát mixed fresh vegetable salad
játra liver
játrová paštika liver pâté

játrové knedlíčky liver dumplings
jazyk tongue
jehněčí lamb
jehněčí kýta leg of lamb
jelení venison
jelito black pudding
jídelní lístek menu
jídla na objednávku dishes to order
jitrnice white pudding (sausage)
jogurt yoghurt

kachna duck
kachna pečená roast duck
kakao cocoa
kapary capers
kapr carp
kapr na černo carp in a black sauce of
  peppercorns and dark beer
kapr na kmíně carp with caraway seeds
kapr na modro carp cooked in stock with wine
  and spices
kapr smažený fried carp
kapusta f cabbage
kapustová polévka cabbage soup
karbanátky rissoles, meatballs, meat loaf,
  hamburgers
kaštany chestnuts
káva coffee
káva bez kofeinu decaffeinated coffee

káva s mlékem coffee with milk
kaviár caviar
kečup ketchup
kedlubna kohlrabi
klobása hot spicy sausage
kmín caraway seed
knedlík s vejcem a okurkou fried bread
  dumpling with eggs and gherkins
knedlíky Czech bread dumplings
koblihy doughnuts
kokos coconut
koláč cake, tart, flan
koláčky sweet buns
kompot stewed fruit
koňak brandy, cognac
koprová omáčka dill sauce
koření seasoning/spice
kotleta cutlet, chop
kozí sýr goat's milk cheese
krab crab
králík rabbit
krém custard, cream
krocan turkey
krokety croquettes
kroupy pearl barley
krůta turkey
krůtí prsa s broskví turkey breast with peach
krvavý biftek rare steak
křen horseradish

křepelka quail
kukuřice sweetcorn
kukuřičné lupínky cornflakes
kulajda a thick soup with potatoes, wild
  mushrooms, dill, egg and sour cream
kuře chicken
kuře s nádivkou roast chicken with chicken
  liver stuffing
kuřecí játra chicken liver
kuře na paprice chicken paprika (spicy)
kuřecí prsa s ananasem chicken breast with
  pineapple
kuřecí rizoto chicken risotto
kuřecí řízek chicken steak/schnitzl
květák cauliflower
kynuté knedlíky s ovocem fruit dumplings
  served with sugar and melted butter
kyselé okurky gherkins
kyselé zelí sauerkraut
kyselý, kyselá, kyselé sour
kýta leg

langoš fried pastry coated in garlic
lasagne lasagne
lázeňské oplatky 'Carlsbad wafers', wafer
  sandwich with walnut or cocoa butter filling
led ice
ledová káva iced coffee
ledvinky kidneys

lesní ovoce fruits of the forest
lihoviny spirits
likér liqueur
lilek aubergine
limonáda lemonade
linecké koláčky latticed jam tarts
lískové ořechy hazelnuts
listový salát green salad
lívanečky pancakes
losos salmon

majolka mayonnaise
majonéza mayonnaise
majoránka marjoram
mák poppy seed
makarony macaroni
makovník cake with poppy seeds
makrela mackerel
maliny raspberries
mandarinka clementine, tangerine, satsuma
mandle almonds
marinovaný(-á/-é) marinated
marmeláda jam
máslo butter
maso meat
masová směs na roštu mixed grill
máta mint
matesy salted herring
mátový čaj mint tea

med honey
meloun watermelon
meruňka apricot
meruňkovice apricot brandy
míchaná vejce scrambled eggs
míchaný salát tossed salad
minerální voda, minerálka mineral water
minutky grilled/short-order dishes
Míša ice lolly made of cottage cheese
mléčná čokoláda milk chocolate
mléčný koktejl milkshake
mléko milk
mleté maso mince
mletý(-á/-é) minced
moravská sudová vína Moravian cask wines
moravský koláč Moravian bun filled twice during
  cooking, first with curd cheese and then jam,
  sprinkled with crumble
moravský vrabec 'Moravian sparrow' - roasted
  pieces of pork sprinkled with caraway seeds
mořské ryby sea fish
mořský krab sea crab
mošt apple juice
moučník sweet, dessert
mouka flour
mražený(-á/-é) frozen
mrkev carrot
mrkvový salát carrot salad
muškátový oříšek nutmeg

nakládaná zelenina pickled vegetables
nakládané houby pickled mushrooms
nakládaný Hermelín camembert-style cheese
  marinated in spices and oil
nanuk ice-cream on a stick
nápoje beverages, drinks
nealkoholické nápoje soft drinks
nektar fruit drink (approx. 10–20% fruit content)
neperlivá voda still water
Niva blue cheese
noky small dumplings/gnocchi
nudle noodles
nudle s mákem sweet noodles with poppy seeds

občerstvení refreshments
oběd lunch, dinner
obilniny cereal
obložený chlebíček small open sandwich
obložený talíř variety platter usually including
  sliced meats, cheeses and vegetables
ocet vinegar
ochutnávka vín wine tasting
okurkový salát cucumber salad
okurky cucumbers, gherkins
olej oil
olivy olives
olomoucké tvarůžky very strong cheese
omáčka sauce
omeleta se zavařeninou jam omelette

opečená klobása roast smoked sausage
ořechový dort walnut cake/gateau
ořechy nuts
ostružiny blackberries
ovar boiled (salted) pork
ovoce fruit
ovocná šťáva fruit juice
ovocné knedlíky fruit dumplings
ovocný čaj fruit tea
ovocný koláč fruit tart
ovocný salát fruit salad

palačinky se šlehačkou a ovocem pancakes
  with fruit and whipped cream
palačinky se špenátem pancakes with spinach
palačinký se zavařeninou pancakes with jam
palačinky se zmrzlinou pancakes with ice cream
pálivá paprika chilli
panák a glass of strong spirits ; a shot
paprika peppers/paprika (spice)
paprikový salám paprika salami
para ořechy Brazil nuts
párátko toothpick
párek sausage/frankfurter
párek v rohlíku hot dog (served in a roll)
paštika pâté
pažitka chives
pečenáč fried herring (eaten cold)
pečený(-á/-é) baked, roasted

pečivo bread, rolls
pepř pepper (spice)
perlivá voda sparkling water
perník gingerbread
petržel parsley
pistácie pistachio nuts
piškot sponge cake, sponge fingers
pivní sýr beer cheese
pivo beer
platýz plaice
plněná vejce hard boiled eggs with tartare sauce
plněné papriky peppers filled with mince
plněný(-á/-é) stuffed/filled
pohár ice-cream sundae
polévky soups
Poličan kind of hard spicy salami
polosuché medium-dry
polotovary ready-to-cook food
pomazánka spread
pomeranč orange
pórek leek
pórková polévka leek soup
povidla thick plum jam
pražská šunka Prague ham
předkrmy starters, appetizers
přílohy side orders/extras
přírodní řízek cutlet
pstruh trout
pstruh na másle trout sautéed in herb butter

punč punch (drink)

rajčatový džus tomato juice
rajčata tomatoes
rajská omáčka tomato sauce
rajská polévka tomato soup
rajčatový/rajčatový salát tomato salad
rebarbora/reveň rhubarb
rizoto risotto
rohlík roll, bread roll
roláda Swiss roll
roštěná entrecôte
rozinky raisins
rum rum
růžičková kapusta Brussels sprouts
růžové víno rosé wine
rybí filé fish fillet
rybí polévka fish soup
rybí salát fish salad
rybíz redcurrant
ryby fish
rýže stewed rice
ředkvičky radishes
řezané pivo black and tan beer
řízek escalope/Wiener schnitzel served mostly
  with potatoes

sachr dort Sachertorte (rich chocolate cake)
salám salami

salát salad/lettuce

salátová okurka cucumber

sardinky sardines

segedínský guláš pork goulash with sauerkraut
in cream sauce

sekaná meatloaf

sekt sparkling wine like champagne

sezam sesame

skopové mutton

skořice cinnamon

sladká paprika sweet peppers

sladkokyselý sweet-and-sour

sladký sweet

slanina s vejci bacon and eggs

slaný savoury, salty

sleď herring

sleď v marinádě marinated herring

slepice na paprice chicken paprika

slepičí vývar s nudlemi chicken broth with
vermicelli

slivovice plum brandy

slunečnicový chléb wholemeal bread with
sunflower seeds

smažené karbanátky fried meatballs/burgers

smažené krokety fried potato croquettes

smažené rybí filé fried fish fillet

smažené žampiony fried mushrooms

smaženice scrambled eggs with wild mushrooms

smažený Hermelín fried camembert-type cheese

smažený kapr carp fried in breadcrumbs
smažený květák fried breaded cauliflower
smažený sýr fried cheese (usually Edam)
smažený vepřový řízek breaded pork
  Wienerschnitzl
smetana cream
smetanový syr cream cheese
snídaně breakfast
sodovka soda water
sójové boby soya beans
sójové maso soya meat
specialita speciality
spišské párky spicy frankfurters
srnčí venison
srnčí hřbet na víně saddle of venison braised
  with wine
sterilované zelí pickled cabbage (not as sour
  as sauerkraut)
strouhanka breadcrumbs
studená kuchyně cold food
studený nářez cold meat platter
studený(-á/-é) cold
sůl salt
sušené ovoce dried fruit
sušené švestky prunes
sušenky biscuits
svačina snack
svařené víno mulled wine
světlé pivo light beer

svíčková na smetaně roast sirloin of beef
 in cream sauce
svítek baked pancake
syrečky beer cheese
syrový(-á/-é) raw
sýr cheese
sýrový talíř cheese platter with various cheeses

šalvěj sage
šampaňské champagne
šípkový čaj rosehip tea
šlehačka f whipped cream
škubánky potato dumplings usually served with
 poppy seeds, melted butter and sugar
škvarky diced bacon
šlehačka whipped cream
šnek snail
šopský salát tomato, pepper and cucumber salad
 with feta-style cheese
špagety spaghetti
španělský ptáček beef olive (beef roll stuffed with
 eggs, bacon and gherkins)
špek hard bacon fat
špekáček a plump sausage, usually grilled or
 roasted over an open fire
špenát spinach
špíz on a skewer
šťáva gravy/juice
štika pike

šunka ham
šunka od kosti sliced ham
šunka s vejci ham and eggs
šunková rolka ham roll usually with a creamy
  filling
švestkový koláč damson tart/plum pie
švestky plums
švestkové knedlíky plum dumplings

tatarský biftek beef tartare
tatarská omáčka tartare sauce
tavený sýr cheese spread
telecí veal
telecí kotlet veal cutlet
telecí řízek veal escalope
teplá jídla hot dishes
teplý(-á/-é) warm
těstoviny pasta
tlačenka pork meatloaf/pie (served with vinegar
  and fresh onion)
tmavé pivo dark beer
točená zmrzlina soft-serve ice cream
točené pivo beer on tap
topinka fried bread usually served with fresh garlic
toust toast
tradiční česká kuchyně traditional Czech cuisine
trubičky se šlehačkou puff pastry cream horns
třešně cherries
tuk fat

tuňák tuna fish
turecká káva Turkish coffee
turistický salám popular cheap salami
tvaroh cottage cheese
tvarohové knedlíky cottage cheese dumplings
tvarohový koláč cheesecake
tykev pumpkin, squash
tymián thyme

ubrousek napkin
uherský salám Hungarian salami
úhoř eel
umělé sladidlo sweetener
ústřice oysters
utopence pickled sausage with onions
uzená šunka smoked ham
uzenáč kipper
uzená makrela smoked mackerel
uzené maso boiled smoked pork
uzeniny smoked foods
uzený jazyk smoked tongue
uzený sýr smoked cheese
uzený(-á/-é) smoked

vafle waffle
vaječná jídla egg dishes
vaječná topinka fried bread with egg and grated
  cheese
vaječný koňak advocaat

vaječný salát egg mayonnaise salad
vanilka vanilla
vanilková zmrzlina vanilla ice-cream
vánočka sweet Christmas bread
vánoční pečivo sweets eaten at Christmas
vařené brambory boiled potatoes
vařený(-á/-é) boiled
vdolky fried doughnut-like bun topped with thick
  plum jam and cottage cheese or whipped cream
večeře dinner, supper
vegetariánská jídla vegetarian dishes
vejce na měkko soft-boiled eggs
vejce na tvrdo hard-boiled eggs
velikonoční mazanec sweet Easter (paschal)
  bread
velikonoční vajíčka Easter eggs
vepřová kotleta pork chop
vepřová krkovice neck of pork
vepřová pečeně se zelím roast pork with
  sauerkraut
vepřové pork
vepřové žebírko stewed rib of pork
vepřový guláš pork goulash
vepřový řízek breaded pork steak/Wiener schnitzl
vídeňská káva Viennese coffee (coffee with
  whipped cream)
vídeňská roštěná entrecôte with onion
vinný lístek wine list
vinný střik wine spritzer

víno wine
višně morello cherries
vlašské ořechy walnuts
vlašský salát a mayonnaise-based salad with
  salami and vegetables
voda water
volské oko fried egg
vývar clear soup

zajíc hare
zajíc na černo stewed hare in thick dark sweet
  sauce with raisins
zajíc na divoko hare cooked with onion, herbs
  and vegetables in red wine
zákusek dessert, sweet, pudding
zálivka dressing
zapečené těstoviny pasta au gratin
zavařenina jam, conserve
zavařený(-á/-é) bottled
zavináč rollmop
zázvor ginger
zelené fazolky green beans
zelenina vegetables
zeleninová polévka vegetable soup
zeleninová obloha garnished with vegetables
zeleninové rizoto vegetable risotto
zeleninový talíř mixed vegetables
zelený čaj green tea
zelí cabbage

zelná polévka (s klobásou) cabbage soup (with smoked sausage)
zmrzlina ice cream
zmrzlinový pohár ice cream sundae
znojemská pečeně slices of roast beef in a gherkin sauce
znojemská roštěná fried sirloin stewed with onions
zvěřina game
zvěřinový guláš game stew

žampióny mushrooms
žebírko spare-rib
želé jelly
žvýkačka f **chewing gum**

Grammar

Nouns

••

Czech nouns, unlike English ones, can be masculine (m), feminine (f) or neuter (nt), regardless of what they mean; for instance, the word for 'girl' is neuter (see below). The genders of nouns are given in the Czech–English dictionary section. In English most words add '-s' in the plural, but in Czech there are several different endings. Here are a few examples.

Masculine nouns usually end in a consonant, e.g.

muž	→ man	**muži**	→ men
hrad	→ castle	**hrady**	→ castles

Feminine nouns usually end in a or e, e.g.

žena	→ woman	**ženy**	→ women
ulice	→ street	**ulice**	→ streets

Neuter nouns usually end in o, e or í, e.g.

město	→ town	**města**	→ towns
děvče	→ girl	**děvčata**	→ girls

Czech has no definite article like 'the' or indefinite article like 'a, an', but the words **ten**, **ta**, **to**, **ti**, **ty** and **ta** are sometimes used for emphasis, like 'this' and 'that' in English, e.g.

ten muž	this man	**ti muži**	these men
ta žena	this woman	**ty ženy**	these women
to město	this town	**ta města**	these towns

One of the complications of Czech is that nouns and adjectives appear with different endings according to the part they play in the sentence (their case). For instance, 'Prague' is **Praha** but 'to Prague' is **do Prahy**, while 'in Prague' is **v Praze** and 'from Prague' is **z Prahy**. In the dictionary section we give nouns and adjectives in the nominative form, but don't be surprised to come across the same word with different endings in different contexts. There are seven cases in all.

Adjectives

Adjectives agree with the noun they refer to, i.e. their endings change according to the noun's gender (masculine, feminine or neuter), number (singular or plural) and case (function in the sentence).

The most common endings in the singular are –ý (masculine), –á (feminine) and –é (neuter). In Czech, as in English, the adjective goes in front of the noun.

masculine	starý muž	the old man
feminine	krásná žena	the beautiful woman
neuter	mladé děvče	the young girl

My, your, his, her

The words for my, your, his, her, etc. also agree with the noun they accompany, e.g.

masculine	feminine	neuter	
můj	moje	moje	my
tvůj	tvoje	tvoje	your (singular/ informal)
jeho	jeho	jeho	his/its
její	její	její	her
náš	naše	naše	our
váš	vaše	vaše	your (plural/ polite)
jejich	jejich	jejich	their

Here are some examples of how the word for 'my' changes according to the part it plays in the sentence:

můj přítel žije v Praze	→	my friend lives in Prague
dům mého přítele	→	the house of my friend
napsal mému příteli	→	he's written to my friend

Pronouns

••

Here are some of the possible forms:

subject		object	
já	I	mě	me
ty	you	tebe/tobě	you
on	he	jeho/ho	him
ona	she	ji/ní	her
ono	it	to/tomu	it
my	we	nás/nám	us
vy	you	vás/vám	you
oni/ony	they	je/ně	them

In Czech, personal pronouns are usually omitted
before verbs, since the verb ending is enough to
indicate the person. They are used only to
emphasize the person or to establish the sex of
the person or the gender of the thing referred to
(if this isn't clear from the context), i.e. 'he', 'she'
or 'it' e.g.

Prší → It's raining.

'You'

There are two ways of addressing people in Czech, depending on their age, how well you know them and how formal or informal the relationship is. **Vy** is the polite word for 'you', and **ty** is the familiar word, which people use when they know each other well. As a tourist you should stick to using **vy**.

Vy is also used for the plural, i.e. when addressing more than one person.

Verbs

Among the most common verbs are **být** (to be), **chtít** (to want), **mít** (to have) and **jít** (to go). Here they are in the present tense:

být	(to be)	chtít	(to want)
(já) jsem	I am	chci	I want
(ty) jsi	you are	chceš	you want
(on/ona/ ono) je	(s)he, it is	chce	(s)he, it wants
(my) jsme	we are	chceme	we want
(vy) jste	you are	chcete	you want
(oni) jsou	they are	chtějí	they want

mít	(to have)	jít	(to go)
(já) mám	I have	jdu	I go
(ty) máš	you have	jdeš	you go
(on/ona/ ono) má	(s)he, it has	jde	(s)he, it goes
(my) máme	we have	jdeme	we go
(vy) máte	you have	jdete	you go
(oni) mají	they have	jdou	they go

To make a verb negative you put **ne** in front of it:

rozumím	I understand
nerozumím	I don't understand
vím	I know
nevím	I don't know
mluvím česky	I speak Czech
nemluvím česky	I don't speak Czech

Past tense

In the past tense, the verb agrees with its subject in gender (masculine, feminine or neuter) and number (singular or plural). You will come across this in the phrases where we include the feminine ending for the past tense, for example:

já jsem byl(a)	→	I was (**byl** = masculine, **byla** = feminine)

Asking questions

●●●●●●●●●●●●●●●●●●●●●●●●●●●●●●●●●●●●●●

To make a yes/no question in Czech you don't need
any extra words; all you need to do is raise your
voice at the end of the sentence, as you might
do informally in English: 'you speak English?'

Mluvíte anglicky?	Do you speak English?
Máte med?	Do you have any honey?

To ask a question to which the answer is not yes or
no, you simply put the relevant word at the begin-
ning of the sentence, as if you were to say 'how
much this is?':

Kolik to stojí?	How much is this?

Public holidays

•••

There are 12 bank holidays in the Czech Republic.
Except for Easter Monday, their dates are fixed.

January 1st	**Nový rok**	
	New Year	
	Restoration of the Czech Independent State (separation of the Czech Republic and Slovakia, 1993)	
March/April	**Velikonoční pondělí**	
	Easter Monday	
May 1st	**Svátek práce**	
	May Day/Labour Day	
May 8th	**Den osvobození**	
	Liberation from Fascism (1945)	
July 5th	**Svátek Cyrila a Metoděje**	
	Saints Cyril and Methodius Day (Christianity introduced, 9th century)	
July 6th	**Den upálení Mistra Jana Husa**	
	Jan Hus (John Huss) burnt at the stake (1415)	
September 28th	**Den české státnosti**	
	Czech Statehood Day	

October 28th	**Den vzniku československé republiky**
	Founding of the Czechoslovak Republic (1918)
November 17th	**Den boje za svobodu a demokracii**
	Freedom and Democracy Day
December 24th	**Štědrý den**
	Christmas Eve (Christmas is celebrated in the evening)
December 25th	**1. svátek vánoční**
	Christmas Day
December 26th	**2. svátek vánoční**
	Boxing Day

Public holidays

English – Czech

A		
a noun	see GRAMMAR	
able: *be able to*	schopný, být schopen	skhop-**nee**, beet skho-pen
abroad: *be abroad*	být v cizině	beet v tsi-zi-n^ye,
go abroad	jet do ciziny	yet do tsi-zi-ni
about	o: okolo	o; o-ko-lo
above	nad	nad
to accept	přijmout	p^rzhiy-mo^wt
do you accept credit cards?	přijímáte platební karty?	p^rzhi-**yee-ma**-te pla-teb-**nee** kar-ti?
access	přístup	p^rzhees-toop
accident	nehoda	ne-ho-da
accommodation	ubytování	oo-bi-to-va-**nee**
account	účet	**oo**-chet
ache: *it aches*	bolí to	bo-**lee** to
address	adresa	ad-re-sa
what's your address?	jaká je vaše adresa?	**ya-ka** ye va-she ad-re-sa?

here's my address	to je moje adresa	to ye mo-ye ad-re-sa
admission	vstupné	vstoop-**ne**
adult	dospělý(-á/-é)	dos-p^ye-**lee** (-**a**/-**e**)
advance: *do I pay in advance?*	platí se předem?	pla-**tee** se p^rzhe-dem?
aeroplane	letadlo	le-tad-lo
after	po	po
afternoon	odpoledne	od-po-led-ne
this afternoon	toto odpoledne	to-to od-po-led-ne
in the afternoon	odpoledne	od-po-led-ne
tomorrow	zítra	**zeet**-ra
afternoon	odpoledne	od-po-led-ne
again	znovu	zno-voo
age	věk	v^yek
ago	před	p^rzhed

English	Czech	Pronunciation
to agree	souhlasit	soW-hla-sit
air conditioning	klimatizace	kli-ma-ti-za-tse
is there air conditioning?	je tam klimatizace?	ye tam kli-ma-ti-za-tse?
airport	letiště	le-tish-tYe
air ticket	letenka	le-ten-ka
alarm clock	budík	boo-**deek**
alcohol	alkohol	al-ko-hol
all (everybody)	všichni	vshikh-ni
(everything)	všechno	vshekh-no
allergic to	alergický (-á/-e) na	aler-gits-**kee** (-**a**/-**e**) na
all right	v pořádku	v po-**zhad**-koo
are you all right?	jste v pořádku?	yste v po-**zhad**-koo?
almost	skoro	sko-ro
alone	sám	sam
also	taky	ta-ki
always	vždy	vzh-di
am: *I am*	jsem; see GRAMMAR	ysem; see GRAMMAR
a.m.	dopoledne	do-po-led-ne
ambulance	sanitka	sa-nit-ka
America	Amerika	a-me-ri-ka
American (person) (m/f)	Američan(ka)	a-me-ri-chan(-ka)
American adj	americký (-á/-é)	a-me-rits-**kee** (-**a**/-**e**)
amount	množství	mnozh-stvee
and	a	a
angry	rozzlobený (-á/-é)	roz-lo-be-**nee** (-**a**/-**e**)
to announce	oznámit	oz-**na**-mit
another: *another beer*	ještě jedno pivo	yesh-tYe yed-no pi-vo
answer noun	odpověď	od-po-vYedY
there's no answer (phone)	nikdo to nebere	nik-do to ne-be-re
to answer	odpovídat	od-po-**vee**-dat
answer phone	záznamník	zaz-nam-**neek**

English – Czech

English – Czech

antibiotics	antibiotika	an-ti-bi-o-ti-ka	apricots	meruňky	me-roon^y-ki

English	Czech	Pronunciation	English	Czech	Pronunciation
antibiotics	antibiotika	an-ti-bi-o-ti-ka	apricots	meruňky	me-roon^y-ki
I'm on antibiotics	beru antibiotika	be-roo an-ti-bi-o-ti-ka	April	duben	du-ben
I need antibiotics	potřebuji antibiotika	pot-rzhe-boo-yi an-ti-bi-o-ti-ka	are	see GRAMMAR	
antifreeze	nemrznoucí směs	ne-mrz-noW-tsee smn/Yes	to arrange	zařídit	za-rhee-dit
antiques	starožitnosti	sta-ro-zhit-nos-ti	arrivals (airport)	přílety	przhee-le-ti
antiseptic	dezinfekce	de-zin-fek-tse	(train)	příjezdy	przhee-yez-di
any (some)	nějaký(-á/-é)	n^ye-ya-kee (-a/-e)	to arrive	přiletět,	przhi-le-t^yet,
				přijet	przhi-yet
I haven't any money	nemám peníze	ne-mam pe-nee-ze	art	umění	oo-mn^ye-nee
apartment	byt	bit	artist m/f	umělec/	oo-mn^ye-lets/
appendix	slepé střevo	sle-pe strzhe-vo		umělkyně	oo-mn^yel-ki-n^ye
apples	jablka	ya-bl-ka	to ask (about)	zeptat se	zep-tat-se
appointment	schůzka	skhooz-ka	(for)	požádat	po-zha-dat
I have an appointment	jsem objednán(a)	ysem ob-yed-nan(-a)	aspirin	acylpyrin	a-sil-pi-rin
do I need an appointment?	musím se objednat?	moo-seem se ob-yed-nat?	asthma	astma	ast-ma
			I get asthma	dostávám astma	dos-ta-vam ast-ma
			at	v	v; see GRAMMAR
			at once	najednou	na-yed-noW
			to attack	napadnout	na-pad-noWt

English	Czech	Pronunciation
attack noun	útok	oo-tok
heart attack	infarkt	in-farkt
August	srpen	sr-pen
Australia	Austrálie	aᵂ-stra-li-ye
Australian	Australan	aᵂ-stra-lan
automatic	automatickou	aᵂ-to-s
car	převodovkou	aᵂ-to-ma-tits-koᵂ pᵇzhe-vo-dov-koᵂ
autumn	podzim	pod-zim
available	k dispozici	k dis-po-zi-tsi
away: *go away!*	běžte pryč!	bᵉezh-te prich!
awful	strašný(-á/-é)	strash-**nee**(-**a**/-**e**)
B		
baby	nemluvně	nem-loov-nᵉe
baby food	potrava pro nemluvňata	pot-ra-va pro-nem-luv-nᵘa-ta
baby-sitter	baby-sitter	bey-bi-si-tr

English	Czech	Pronunciation
back (of body)	záda	za-da
back: *when will he/she be back?*	kdy bude zpátky?	kdi boo-de zpat-ki?
he/she is back	je zpátky	ye zpat-ki
bad (spoiled)	zkažený (-á/-é);	zka-zhe-**nee** (-**a**/-**e**);
(otherwise)	špatný	shpat-**nee**
bag	taška	tash-ka
baggage	zavazadla	za-va-zad-la
baker's	pekařství	pe-kaᵇzhst-**vee**
bank	banka	ban-ka
bank account	bankovní konto	ban-kov-**nee** kon-to
bar	bar	bar
bathroom	koupelna	koᵂ-pel-na
battery	baterie	ba-te-ri-ye
be	see GRAMMAR	
beautiful	krásný(-á/-é)	kras-**nee**(-**a**/-**e**)
because	protože	pro-to-zhe
bed	postel	pos-tel

164 | 165

English – Czech

English	Czech	
bedroom	ložnice	lozh-ni-tse
beer	pivo	pi-vo
a beer, please	jedno pivo, prosím	yed-no pi-vo pro-**seem**
before	před	p**zhed**
before dinner	před večeří	p**zhed** ve-che-**rzhee**
to begin	začít	za-**cheet**
behind/	za	za
beyond		
to believe	věřit	vye-**rzhit**
below	pod	pod
beside (next to)	vedle	ved-le
best	nejlepší	ney-lep-**shee**
better (than)	lepší (než)	lep-**shee** (nezh)
between	mezi	me-zi
bicycle	kolo	ko-lo
big	velký(-á/-é)	vel-**kee**(-a/-e)
bigger	větší	v**yet**-shee
biggest	největší	ney-v**yet**-shee
bill	účet	**oo**-chet

English	Czech	
the bill, please	účet, prosím	**oo**-chet, pro-**seem**
birthday	narozeniny	na-ro-ze-ni-ni
happy birthday	všechno nejlepší k narozeninám	vshe-khno ney-lep-shee k na-ro-ze-ni-**nam**
birthday card	přání k narozeninám	p**zha**-**nee**k na-ro-ze-ni-**nam**
biscuits	sušenky	soo-shen-ki
bit: *a bit*	trochu	tro-khoo
bite noun (insect)	bodnutí	bod-noo-**tee**
(dog)	kousnutí	koWs-noo-**tee**
bitter (taste)	hořký(-á/-é)	hoZh-**kee**(-a/-e)
black	černý(-á/-é)	cher-**nee**(-a/-e)
bleed	krvácet	kr-**va**-tset
blind adj (person)	slepý(-á/-é)	sle-**pee**(-a/-e)
blood	krev	krev
blood group	krevní skupina	krev-**nee** skoo-pi-na
blue	modrý(-á/-é)	mod-**ree**(-a/-e)

boarding card	palubní lístek	pa-lub-**nee** **lees**-tek
boat trip	výlet lodí	**vee**-let lo-**dee**
body	tělo	**tYe**-lo
boiled (food)	uvařený(-á/-é)	oo-va-**rzhe**-nee (-**a**/-**é**)
book noun	kniha	**kni**-ha
guidebook	průvodce	**proo**-vod-tse
to book	zamluvit si	zam-**loo**-vit si
booking office	pokladna	pok-**lad**-na
bookshop	knihkupectví	knih-koo-**pets**-tvee
boring: it's boring	je to nudné	ye to **nood**-ne
born: to be born	narodit se	na-ro-**dit**-se
to borrow	vypůjčit si	vi-**pooy**-chit si
both	oba	**o**-ba
bottle	láhev	**la**-hev
a bottle of water	láhev vody	**la**-hev **vo**-di
box office	pokladna	pok-**lad**-na
boy	chlapec	khla-pets
boyfriend	přítel	p'**zhee**-tel
to brake	brzdit	brz-dit
brakes noun	brzdy	brz-di
bread	chleba	khle-ba
to break	rozbit	roz-**beet**
breakfast	snídaně	snee-da-nYe
what time is breakfast?	v kolik hodin je snídaně?	v ko-lik ho-din ye snee-da-nYe?
breast (person)	prsa	prr-sa
(chicken)	prsíčka	prr-**seech**-ka
to breathe	dýchat	**dee**-khat
brewery	pivovar	pi-vo-var
bridge (road, etc.)	most	most
briefcase	kufřík; aktovka	?????; ak-tov-ka
to bring	přinést	p'zhi-**nest**
Britain	Británie	bri-**ta**-ni-ye
British adj	britský(-á/-é)	brits-**kee**(-**a**/-**e**)
broken	rozbité	roz-bi-**te**
broken: it's broken	je to rozbité	ye to roz-bi-**te**

English – Czech

broken down (car)	rozbilo se	roz-bi-lo se	by train	vlakem	vla-kem
brother	bratr	bra-tr	by car	autem	aw-tem
brown	hnědý(-á/-é)	hnye-**dee**(-**a**/-**e**)	bye bye	ahoj	a-hoy
buffet car	jídelní vůz	yee-del-nee **vooz**			
bulb (light)	žárovka	zha-rov-ka	**C**		
burglary	vloupání	vloW-**pa**-nee	café	kavárna	ka-**var**-na
bus	autobus	aW-to-boo-so-ve	cake	zákusek;	za-koo-sek;
bus station	autobusové nádraží	aW-to-boo-so-ve nad-ra-**zhee**		koláč; dort	ko-**lach**; dort
bus stop	autobusová zastávka	aW-to-boo-so-**va** zas-**tav**-ka	to call (on phone)	telefonovat	te-le-fo-no-vat
			call noun (phone)	telefonický hovor	te-le-fo-nits-**kee** ho-vor
bus ticket	jízdenka	**yeez**-den-ka	camcorder	videokamera	vi-de-o-ka-me-ra
busy	rušný,	**roosh**-nee,	camera	fotoaparát	fo-to-a-pa-**rat**
	zaměstnaný (-á/-é)	za-mnYest-na-**nee**(-**a**/-**e**)	camp site	kemp	kemp
I'm busy	mám moc práce	mam mots pra-tse	can: can I…?	mohu…?	mo-hoo…?
			I cannot	nemohu	ne-mo-hoo
butter	máslo	mas-lo	Canada	Kanada	ka-na-da
to buy	koupit	koW-pit	Canadian	kanadský (-á/-é)	ka-nad-skee (-**a**/-**e**)
by: by bus	autobusem	aW-to-boo-sem	to cancel	zrušit	zroo-shit

English	Czech	pronunciation
I want to cancel my booking	chci zrušit rezervaci	khtsi zroo-shit re-zer-va-tsi
capital	hlavní město	hlav-**nee** mn**Yes**-to
car	auto	a**W**-to
car insurance	pojištění	por-yish-t**Ye**-**nee**
car park	parkoviště	par-ko-vish-t**Ye**
car wash	myčka aut	**mich**-ka a**W**t
card (greetings)	pohled	po-hled
(playing) cards	karty	**kar**-ti
business card	vizitka	vi-**zit**-ka
credit card	kreditní karta	kre-dit-**nee kar**-ta
to be careful	být opatrný	beet opa-tr-**nee**
carriage (of train)	železniční vagón	zhe-lez-nich-**nee** va-**gon**
carrots	mrkve	**mrk**-ve
to carry	nosit	**no**-sit
case	kufr	**koo**-fr
cash noun	hotovost	**ho**-to-vost
cash desk	pokladna	pok-**lad**-na
cash machine	bankomat	**ban**-ko-mat
castle	hrad	hrad
casualty department	oddělení úrazů	od-d**Ye**-le-nee **oo**-ra-**zoo**
cat	kočka	**koch**-ka
to catch (bus, train, etc.)	stihnout	sti-hno**W**t
cathedral	katedrála	ka-ted-**ra**-la
Catholic	katolický (-á/-é)	ka-to-lits-**kee** (-**a**/-**e**)
cauliflower	květák	kv**Ye**-**tak**
CD	CD	**tse**-de
celery	řapíkový celer	**r**zha-**pee**-ko-**vee** tse-ler
cell phone	mobil	mo-**bil**
centimetre	centimetr	tsen-ti-me-tr
central heating	ústřední topení	**oos**-t**rzhed**-nee to-pe-**nee**
central	centrální	tsen-**tral**-nee
locking (car)	zamykání	za-mi-ka-**nee**

English – Czech

English	Czech	pronunciation
centre	střed	střhed
town centre	střed města	střhed mnYes-ta
cereal	cereálie, obiloviny	tse-re-a-li-ye, o-bi-lo-vi-ni
certificate	potvrzení	pot-vr-ze-**nee**
chain (jewellery)	řetízek	řzhe-**tee**-zek
chair	židle	zhid-le
champagne	šampaňské	sham-pany-skee
change n (coins)	drobné	drob-**nee**
to change	vyměnit	vi-mnYe-nit
where can I	kde si mohu	kde si mo-hoo
change	vyměnit	vi-mnYe-nit
money?	peníze?	pe-**nee**-ze?
do I have to	musím	moo-sim
change? (train)	přesedat?	pžhe-se-dat?
charge (fee) noun	poplatek	po-pla-tek
charge it to	připište mi to	pžhi-pish-te mi to
my account	k účtu	to **kooch**-too
to charge (mobil)	nabít	na-**beet**
cheap	levný(-á/-é)	lev-**nee**(-**a**/-**e**)
cheaper	levnější	lev-nYey-**shee**
cheap rate (phone)	zlevněná sazba	zlev-nYe-**na** saz-ba
to check	kontrolovat	kon-tro-lo-vat
to check in (at hotel)	ubytovat se	oo-bi-to-vat se
cheers!	na zdraví!	na zdra-**veel**
cheese	sýr	seer
chemist's (pharmacy)	lékárna	le-**kar**-na
cheque	drogerie	dro-**ge**-ri-ye
cheque card (for cosmetics)	šek	shek
cherries	šeková karta	she-ko-va kar-ta
chest (of body)	třešně	tžhesh-nYe
chewing gum	hruď	hroody
chicken	žvýkačka	zhvee-kach-ka
child	kuře	koo-žzhe
children	dítě	dee-tYe
chips	děti	dYe-ti
chocolate	hranolky	hra-nol-ki
	čokoláda	cho-ko-**la**-da

English	Czech	
hot chocolate	horká čokoláda	hor-**ka** cho-ko-**la**-da
choose: can I choose?	mohu si vybrat?	**mo**-hoo si vib-rat?
Christmas	Vánoce	va-no-tse
Merry Christmas!	veselé Vánoce!	ve-se-le va-no-tse!
church	kostel, cirkev	kos-tel, tseer-kev
Protestant church	protestantský kostel	pro-tes-tants-**kee** kos-tel
cigarettes	cigarety	tsi-ga-re-ti
a packet of cigarettes	balíček cigaret	ba-**lee**-chek tsi-ga-ret
cigarette lighter	zapalovač	za-pa-lo-vach
cinema	kino	ki-no
what's on at the cinema?	co se hraje v kině?	tso se hra-ye v ki-nYe?
city	město	mnYes-to
clean adj	čistý(-á/-é)	chis-**tee**(-**a**/-**e**)
to clean	vyčistit; uklidit	vi-chis-tit; ook-li-dit
to climb (stairs)	jít po schodech, lézt	yeet po skho-dekh, lezt
clock	hodiny	ho-di-ni
to close	zavírat	za-**vee**-rat
closed (shop)	zavřený(-á/-é)	zav-zhe-**nee** (-**a**/-**e**)
clothes	oblečení	o-ble-che-**nee**
cloudy	oblačno	ob-lach-no
coach	zataženo	za-ta-zhe-no
coat	autobus	a^w-to-boos
cocoa	kabát	ka-**bat**
coffee	kakao	ka-ka-o
black coffee	káva	**ka**-va
iced coffee	černá káva	cher-**na ka**-va
coin	ledová káva	le-do-**va ka**-va
cold (illness)	mince	min-tse
cold noun	nachlazení	nakh-la-ze-**nee**
I have a cold	rýma	**ree**-ma
	mám rýmu	**mam ree**-moo

English – Czech

English	Czech		English	Czech	
cold adj	studený(-á/-é)	stu-de-**nee** (**-a/-e**)	to complete	dokončit	do-kon-chit
I'm cold	je mi zima	ye mi zi-ma	computer	počítač	po-**chee**-tach
it's cold (weather)	je zima	ye zi-ma	condoms	kondomy	kon-do-mi
to collect (someone)	vyzvednout	viz-ved-no^wt,	conference	konference	kon-fe-ren-tse
colour	sbírat	s**ee**-rat	to confirm (flight)	potvrdit	po-tvr-dit
coloured;	barva	bar-va	confused	nejasný(-á/-é)	ne-yas-**nee** (**-a/-e**)
in colour;	barevný	ba-rev-**nee**	congratu-lations!	blahopřeji!	bla-ho-p**zhe**-yi!
colourful	(**-á/-é**)	(**-a/-e**)			
to come (arrive)	přijít	p'zhi-**yeet**	connection (train, plane)	spojení	spo-ye-**nee**
come in!	dále, vstupte!	????, **vstoop-te!**	contact lens	kontaktní čočka	kon-takt-nee choch-ka
comfortable	pohodlný (**-á/-é**)	po-ho-dl-**nee** (**-a/-e**)	to continue	pokračovat	po-kra-cho-vat
company (business)	firma, společnost	fir-ma, spo-lech-nost	contraceptives	antikoncepce	an-ti-kon-tsep-tse
compartment (on train)	kupé	koo-**pe**	contract	smlouva	smlow-va
			convenient	výhodný	vee-hod-**nee**
to complain	stěžovat si	st'e-zho-vat si	to cook	vařit	va-**zhit**
complaint	stížnost	steezh-nost	cookies	sušenky	soo-shen-ki

English	Czech	Pronunciation
copy noun	kopie	ko-pi-ye
to copy (photocopy)	kopírovat	ko-**pee**-ro-vat
corner (of street)	roh	roh
cornflakes	kukuřičné lupínky	koo-koo-ř̌zhich-ne loo-**peen**-ki
corridor	chodba	khod-ba
cosmetics	kosmetika	kos-me-ti-ka
to cost	stát	stat
how much does it cost?	kolik to stojí?	**ko**-lik to sto-**yee**?
costume (swimming)	plavky	plav-ki
cotton wool	vata	va-ta
couchette	lehátko	le-**hat**-ko
to cough	kašlat	kash-lat
country	země, venkov	ze-mnye, ven-kov
countryside	venkov	ven-kov
couple (two people)	pár	par
a couple of...	několik	nYe-ko-lik
course (of meal)	chod	khod
crafts	řemesla	ř̌zhe-mes-la
crash (car) noun	náraz	**na**-raz
to crash	narazit, mít nehodu	na-ra-zit, meet ne-ho-doo
cream (for face, etc.)	krém	krem
cream (on milk)	smetana	sme-ta-na
credit card	kreditní karta	kre-dit-**nee** kar-ta
crime	zločin	zlo-chin
crisps	brambůrky	bram-**boor**-ki
to cross (road)	přejít	př̌zhe-**yeet**
cross-country skis	běžky	bYezh-ki
crossroads	křižovatka	kř̌zhi-zho-vat-ka
crowded: will it be crowded?	bude tam plno?	boo-de tam pl-no?
to cry (weep)	plakat	pla-kat
cucumber (not pickled)	okurka	o-koor-ka

English – Czech

English	Czech	Pronunciation
cup	šálek	sha-lek
current (electric)	proud	prowd
customs (duty)	clo	tslo
cut noun	řez	rzhez
to cut	řezat	rzhe-zat
to cycle	jezdit na kole	yez-dit na ko-le
cystitis	cystitida	tsis-ti-ti-da

D

English	Czech	Pronunciation
daily	denně	de-nYe
dairy produce	mléčné výrobky	mlech-ne vee-rob-ki
damage noun	škoda	shko-da
damp	vlhký(-á/-é)	vlh-kee(-a/-e)
dance noun	tanec	ta-nets
to dance	tancovat	tan-tso-vat
danger	nebezpečí	ne-bez-pe-chee
dangerous	nebezpečný (-á/-é)	ne-bez-pech-nee (-a/-e)
dark	tmavý(-á/-é)	tma-vee(-a/-e)
date (day)	datum	da-tum
date of birth	datum narození	da-tum na-ro-ze-nee
daughter	dcera	dtse-ra
day	den	den
every day	každý den	kazh-dee den
which day?	který den?	kte-ree den?
dead	mrtvý(-á/-é)	mrrt-vee(-a/-e)
deaf	hluchý(-á/-é)	hloo-khee(-a/-e)
decaffeinated coffee	káva bez kofeinu	ka-va bez ko-fey-noo
have you decaff?	máte kávu bez kofeinu?	ma-te ka-voo bez ko-fey-noo?
December	prosinec	pro-si-nets
deck chair	lehátko	le-hat-ko
to declare	proclit	pro-tsleet
nothing to declare	nic k proclení	nits k pro-tsle-nee
deep	hluboký(-á/-é)	hloo-bo-kee (-a/-e)
delay noun	zpoždění	zpozh-dYe-nee

English	Czech	Pronunciation
what's the delay?	jaké to má zpoždění?	ya-**kee** to ma zpozh-dye-**nee**?
delayed (flight, train)	zpožděný (-á/-é)	zpozh-dye-**nee** (-á/-é)
delicious	lahodný(-á/-é)	la-hod-**nee** (-á/-é)
dental floss	dentální nit'	den-**tál**-nee nitY
dentist (m/f)	zubař(ka)	zoo-**bazh**(-ka)
deodorant	dezodorant	de-zo-do-rant
to depart	odjet	od-yet
(plane)	odletět	od-le-tYet
(walk)	odejit	o-de-yit
department store	obchodní dům	ob-khod-**nee** doom
departures	odjezdy	od-yez-di
departure lounge	odjezdová hala	od-yez-do-**va** ha-la
to describe	popsat	pop-sat
description	popis	po-pis

English	Czech	Pronunciation
desk (in an office, bank)	pracovní stůl	pra-tsov-ni **stool**
dessert	zákusek	**za**-koo-sek
details	detaily	de-tay-li
to develop (photos)	vyvolat	vee-vo-lat
diabetic	diabetik/ diabetička	di-a-be-**tik**/ di-a-be-**tichka**
dialling code	předčíslí	pzhed-**chees-lee**
dictionary	slovník	slov-**neek**
to die	zemřít	zem-**Tzheet**
diesel	nafta	naf-ta
diet	dieta	di-ye-ta
I'm on a diet	mám dietu	**mam** di-ye-too
different	jiný(-á/-é)	yi-**nee**(-á/-é)
difficult: *it's difficult*	je to těžké	ye to tYezh-**ke**
digital camera	digitální fotoaparát	di-gi-**tal-nee** fo-to-apa-**rat**
dining room	jídelna	**yee**-del-na
dinner noun	večeře	ve-**che**-zhe

English – Czech

English	Czech	Pronunciation
to have dinner	večeřet	ve-che-rzhet
direct: is it a direct train?	je to přímý vlak?	ye to přzhee-mee vlak
directions	popis cesty	po-pis tses-ti
dirty	špinavý(-á/-é)	shpi-na-vee (-a/-e)
disabled (person)	zdravotně postižený(-á)	zdra-vot-nYe po-sti-zhe-nee (-a)
to disagree	nesouhlasit	ne-soW-hla-sit
to disappear	zmizet	zmi-zet
disaster	katastrofa	ka-tas-tro-fa
disco	diskotéka	dis-ko-te-ka
discount	sleva	sle-va
to discover	objevit	ob-ye-vit
disease	nemoc	ne-mots
disk (floppy disk)	disketa	dis-ke-ta
disposable	na jedno použití	na yed-no pow-zhi-tee
distance	vzdálenost	vzda-le-nost
district (in town)	čtvrť	chtvrty
to disturb	rušit	ru-shit
diversion	objížďka	ob-yeezhdY-ka
divorced (m/f)	rozvedený(-á)	roz-ve-de-nee(-a)
dizzy: I feel dizzy	mám závrať	mam za-vraty
to do	dělat	dYe-lat
doctor (m/f)	doktor(ka)	dok-tor(-ka)
documents	doklady	do-kla-di
dog	pes	pes
dollar	dolar	do-lar
domestic (flight)	domácí	do-ma-tsee
door	dveře	dve-rzhe
double	dvojí, dvojitý(-á/-é)	????? dvo-yi-tee (-a/-e)
double bed	dvoulůžko	dvoW-loozh-ko
double room	pokoj pro dvě osoby	po-koy pro dvě o-so-bi
down	dolů	do-loo
downstairs	dole, dolů	do-le, do-loo
draught: there's a draught	je tu průvan	ye too proo-van

draught beer	čepované pivo	che-po-va-ne pi-vo
dress noun	šaty	sha-ti
to dress (oneself)	obléci se	o-ble-tsi se
dressing (for food)	zálivka	za-liv-ka
drink noun	pití	pi-tee
to drink	pít	peet
to drive	řídit	rzhee-dit
driver (m/f)	řidič(ka)	rzhi-dich(-ka)
driving licence	řidičský průkaz	rzhi-dich-skee proo-kaz
drug (medicine)	lék	lek
drug (narcotics)	droga	dro-ga
drunk	opilý(-á/-é)	o-pi-lee(-a/-e)
to dry	usušit	oo-soo-shit
dry	suchý	soo-khee
dry-clean	vyčistit	vi-chis-tit
dry-cleaner's	čistírna	chis-teer-na
during	během	bye-hem

| DVD | DVD | de ve de |
| DVD player | přehrávač | przhe-hra-vach |

E

each	každý(-á/-é)	kazh-dee(-a/-e)
ear(s)	ucho (uši)	oo-kho (oo-shi)
earache	bolest ucha	bo-lest oo-kha
earlier	dříve	dźhnee-ve
early	brzo	br-zo
earn	vydělat	vi-dYe-lat
earphones	sluchátka	sloo-khat-ka
east	východ	vee-khod
Easter	Velikonoce	ve-li-ko-no-tse
Happy Easter!	Veselé Velikonoce!	ve-se-le ve-li-ko-no-tse!
easy	snadný(-á/-é)	snad-nee(-a/-e)
eat	jíst	yeest
egg	vejce	vey-tse
hard-boiled egg	vejce na tvrdo	vey-tse na tvr-do
scrambled eggs	míchaná vejce	mee-kha-na vey-tse

English	Czech	Pronunciation
either... or	bud'... anebo	budᵛ...a-ne-bo
electric	elektrický (-á/-é)	e-lekt-rits-**kee** (-á/-**e**)
electronic	elektronický (-á/-é)	e-lek-tro-nits-**kee** (-á/-**e**)
e-mail	e-mail	**ee**-meyl
e-mail address	e-mailová adresa	????? ad-re-sa
embassy	velvyslanectví	vel-vi-sla-nets-**tvee**
emergency	naléhavá situace	na-**le**-ha-**va** si-tu-a-tse
emergency exit	nouzový východ	noW-zo-**vee vee**-khod
empty: it's empty	je to prázdné	ye to prazd-**ne**
end: when does it end?	kdy to končí?	kdi to kon-**chee**?
engaged (busy, occupied) (phone, etc.)	obsazený (-á/-é)	ob-sa-ze-**nee** (-á/-**e**)
full; occupied	obsazeno	ob-sa-ze-no
England	Anglie	ang-gli-ye
English (person) (m/f) adj	Angličan(ka)	ang-gli-chan(-ka)
	anglický(-á/-é)	ang-glits-**kee** (-**a**/-**e**)
do you speak English?	mluvite anglicky?	mloo-**vee**-te ang-glits-ki?
enjoy: to enjoy oneself; to have a good time	bavit se	ba-vit se
I enjoy swimming	rád(a) plavu	**ra**d/a pla-voo
enjoy your meal!	dobrou chut'!	dob-roW khooty!
enough: that's enough	to stačí	to sta-**chee**
enquiry desk	informace	in-for-ma-tse
to enter	vstoupit	vstoW-pit
entrance	vchod	vchod

English	Czech	Pronunciation
entrance fee	vstupné	vstoo-pne
equal	stejný(-á/-é)	snad-nee(-a/-é)
equipment	vybavení	vi-ba-ve-nee
error	chyba	khi-ba
escape: *fire escape*	úniková cesta / v případě požáru	**oo**-ni-ko-va / tses-ta v / p'**zhee**-pa-dye po-**zha**-roo
essential	zásadní	za-sad-**nee**
Europe	Evropa	ev-ro-pa
European	evropský (-á/-é)	ev-rop-**skee** (-á/-e)
evening	večer	ve-cher
this evening	dnes večer	dnes ve-cher
tomorrow evening	zítra večer	zi-tra ve-cher
every	každý(-á/-é)	kazh-**dee**(-a/-é)
pl	všichni	vshi-khni
everyone	každý(-á/-é)	kazh-**dee**(-a/-é)
pl	všichni	vshi-khni
everything	všechno	vshekh-no
everywhere	všude	vshoo-de
example	příklad	p'**zhee**-klad
excellent	vynikající	vi-ni-ka-**yee**-tsee
except	kromě	kro-mnye
to exchange	vyměnit	vi-mnye-nit
exchange rate *noun*	kurs	koors
to excuse	prominout, omluvit	pro-mi-no^Wt, o-mloo-vit
excuse me!	promiňte!	pro-min^Y-te!
exercise	cvičení	tsvi-che-**nee**
exhibition	výstava	**vee**-sta-va
exit	východ	**vee**-khod
expensive	drahý(-á/-é)	dra-**hee**(-a/-é)
to expire (ticket, etc.)	pozbýt platnosti	poz-**beet** plat-nos-ti
to explain	vysvětlit	vis-**Vyet**-lit
express train	rychlík	rikh-**leek**
extra	navíc	na-vits
eye(s)	oko (oči)	o-ko (o-chi)

F

English	Czech	Pronunciation
face	obličej	o-bli-chey
facilities (leisure facilities)	zařízení	za-rzhee-ze-nee
to fail	neuspět	neW-spYet
to faint	omdlít	omd-leet
fair (hair)	světlý(-á/-é)	svYet-lee(-a/-e)
fake: this is a fake	to není pravé	to ne-nee pra-ve
fall noun	podzim	pod-zim
to fall	padat	pa-dat
he(she) has fallen	spadl(a)	spa-dl(a)
family	rodina	ro-di-na
far	daleko	da-le-ko
is it far?	je to daleko?	ye-to da-le-ko?
fare (train, bus, etc.)	jízdné	yeez-dnee
fashionable	módní	mod-nee
fast	rychle	rikh-le

English	Czech	Pronunciation
to fasten (seat belt)	připoutat se	pr7zhi-poW-tat se
fat adj	tlustý(-á/-é)	tloos-tee(-a/-e)
father	otec	o-tets
fault (defect)	vada	va-da
it's not my fault	to není moje chyba	to ne-nee mo-ye khi-ba
favour	prosba	pros-ba
favourite	oblíbený (-á/-é)	o-blee-be-nee (-á/-é)
fax	fax	faks
to fax	poslat fax, faxovat	pos-lat faks, fak-so-vat
February	únor	oo-nor
to feel	cítit	tsee-tit
I don't feel well	necítím se dobře	ne-tsee-teem se dob-rzhe
feet	nohy	no-hi
female	žena	zhe-na
to fetch	přinést	przhi-nest
fever	horečka	ho-rech-ka

English	Czech	Pronunciation
few		
a few	málo	ma-lo
to fill (up)	několik	nYe-ko-lik
to fill (in form)	naplnit	na-pl-nit
fillet (steak)	vyplnit	vi-pl-nit
film	filé	fi-le
to find	film	film
fine n (to be paid)	najít	na-yeet
fine adj (weather)	pokuta	po-koo-ta
finger(s)	pěkný(-á/-é)	pYek-nee(-a/-e)
to finish	prst(y)	prst(i)
fire	končit	kon-chit
fire alarm	oheň	o-henY
	požární poplach	po-zhar-nee po-plakh
fire extinguisher	hasicí přístroj	ha-si-chee pYzhe-stroy
firm n (company)	firma, společnost	fir-ma, spo-lech-nost
first	první	prv-nee
first aid	první pomoc	prv-nee po-mots

English	Czech	Pronunciation
first class	první třída	prv-nee třzhee-da
first name	křestní jméno	křzhe-stnee yme-no
fish noun	ryba	rí-ba
to fish	chytat ryby	khi-tat rí-bi
to fit (attack) noun	záchvat	zakh-vat
to fit: it doesn't fit me	nesedí mi to	ne-se-dee mi-to
to fix	opravit	o-pra-vit
can you fix it?	můžete to opravit?	moo-zhe-te to o-pra-vit?
fizzy: is it fizzy?	je to perlivé?	ye to per-li-ve?
flash (for camera)	blesk	blesk
flat noun (apartment)	byt	bit
flat adj	plochý(-á/-é)	plo-khee(-a/-e)
flavour	příchuť	přzhe-khooty
flight	let	let

English – Czech

English	Czech	Pronunciation
floor	poschodí	pos-kho-**dee**
(of building)	patro	pat-ro
(of room)	podlaha	pod-la-ha
flowers	květiny	kvYe-ti-ni
flu	chřipka	khři-pka
to fly	letět	le-tYet
fog	mlha	ml-ha
to fold	přehnout	přzhe-hnoᵘt
to follow	sledovat	sle-do-vat
food	jídlo	yeed-lo
foot (feet)	noha (nohy)	no-ha (no-hi)
on foot	pěšky	pYesh-ki
football (game)	fotbal	fot-bal
for	pro	pro
for me	pro mě	pro mnYe
for you	pro vás	pro vas
for him/her	pro něj/ni	pro nYev/ni
for us	pro nás	pro nas
forbidden	zakázáno	za-**ka**-**za**-no
foreign	cizí	tsi-**zee**
foreigner	cizinec	tsi-zi-nets
forever	navždy	nav-zhdi
to forget	zapomenout	za-po-me-noᵘt
fork (for eating)	vidlička	vid-lich-ka
fork (in road)	rozcestí	roz-tses-tee
fortnight	čtrnáct dní	chtrr-natst dnee
forward(s)	dopředu	do-přzhe-doo
fountain	vodotrysk;	vo-do-trisk;
	fontána	fon-**ta**-na
fracture noun	zlomenina	zlo-me-ni-na
fragile	křehký(-á/-é)	křzheh-**kee**(-**a**/-**e**)
France	Francie	fran-tsi-ye
free (unoccupied)	volný(-á/-é)	vol-**nee**(-**a**/-**e**)
free (costing nothing)	zadarmo	za-dar-mo
French		
(person) (m/f)	Francouz(ka)	fran-tsoᵂs(-ka)
adj	francouzský (-á/-é)	fran-tsoᵂs-**kee** (-**a**/-**e**)
do you speak French?	mluvíte francouzsky?	mloo-**vee**-te fran-tsoᵂs-ki?
frequent	častý(-á/-é)	chas-**tee**(-**a**/-**e**)
Friday	pátek	**pa**-tek

English	Czech	Pronunciation
fried (food)	smažený (-á/-é)	sma-zhe-**nee** (-**a**/-**e**)
fried bread	topinka	to-pin-ka
fried cheese (usually edam)	smažený sýr	sma-zhe-**nee** seer
friend	přítel(kyně)	pzhee-tel (-ki-nYe)
friendly	přátelsky	pzha-tel-ski
from	od, z/ze	od, z/ze
I'm from Scotland	jsem ze Skotska	ysem ze skot-ska
I'm from London	jsem z Londýna	ysem z lon-**dee**-na
front	přední	pzhed-**nee**
can I sit in the front?	mohu sedět vepředu?	mo-hoo se-dYet ve-pzhe-doo?
in front of you	před vámi	pzhed **va**-mi
fruit	ovoce	o-vo-tse
fruit juice	ovocný džus	o-vots-**nee** dzhoos
to fry	smažit	sma-zhit
fuel (petrol)	palivo	pa-li-vo
full	benzin	ben-**zeen**
full (occupied)	plný(-á/-é)	pl-**nee**(-**a**/-**e**)
	obsazený (-á/-é)	ob-sa-ze-**nee** (-**a**/-**e**)
full board	plná penze	pl-na pen-ze
funny (amusing)	legrační;	leg-rach-**nee**;
	veselý(-á/-é)	ve-se-**lee**(-**a**/-**e**)
furnished (with furniture)	zařízený	za-**ízhe**-ze-**nee**
future noun adj	budoucnost	boo-do^Wts-nost,
	budoucí	boo-do^W-tsee
G		
gallery (art)	galerie	ga-le-ri-ye
game (sport)	hra	hra
(meat)	zvěřina	zvYe-**rzhi**-na
garage (private)	garáž	ga-**razh**
(selling petrol, etc.)	benzinová pumpa;	ben-zi-no-**va** poom-pa;
	autopravna	a^W-to-o-prav-na

English	Czech	Pronunciation
garden	zahrada	za-hra-da
gate (at airport)	východ	vee-khod
gents	Muži; Páni	moo-zhi; pa-ni
genuine: is this genuine?	je to pravé?	ye to pra-ve?
German (person) (m/f)	Němec/Němka	nYe-mets/nYem-ka
adj	německý (-á/-é)	nYe-mets-kee (-a/-e)
Germany	Německo	nYe-mets-ko
to get (obtain) (receive)	dostat obdržet	dos-tat ob-dr-zhet
(fetch)	přinést	pzhi-nest
get on/off (bus, etc.)	nastoupit vystoupit	nas-tow-pit, vis-tow-pit
gift	dárek	da-rek
girl	dívka, děvče	deev-ka, dYev-che
to give	dávat	da-vat
(give back)	vrátit	vra-tit
glass (substance)	sklo	sklo
(for drink)	sklenice	skle-ni-tse
a glass of water	sklenice vody	skle-ni-tse vo-di
glasses (spectacles)	brýle	bree-le
to go (on foot)	jít	yeet
(in vehicle)	jet	yet
go back	vrátit se	vra-tit se
go in	vejít	ve-yeet
go out	odejít	o-de-yeet
good	dobrý(-á/-é)	dob-ree(-a/-e)
good	dobré	dob-re
afternoon	odpoledne	od-po-led-ne
goodbye	nashledanou, ahoj	nas-khle-da-now, a-hoy
goodnight	dobrou noc	dob-row nots
gram	gram	gram
grandfather	dědeček	dYe-de-chek
grandmother	babička	ba-bich-ka

grapefruit	grep	grep	o-kroozh-**nee**
grapes	hroznové víno	hroz-no-**ve vee**-no	**yeez**-da
			okružní jízda	guided tour
greasy	mastný(-á/-é)	mast-**nee**(-a/-**e**)	
great	velký(-á/-é)	vel-**kee**(-a/-**e**)	H
	významný	**veez**-nam-**nee**	
	(-á/-é)	(-a/-**e**)	vlasy	hair	vla-si
Great Britain	Velká Británie	vel-ka bri-**ta**-ni-ye	kadeřnictví	hairdresser's	ka-deřzh-**nits-tvee**
green card	zelená karta	ze-le-**na** kar-ta		(for women)	
(car insurance)			polovina;	half	po-lo-vi-na;
greengrocer's	zelenina	ze-le-ni-na	půl		**pool**
(shop)			polopenze	half board	po-lo-pen-ze
grey	šedivý(-á/-é)	she-di-**vee**(-a/-**e**)	půl hodiny	half an hour	**pool** ho-di-ni
grocer's (shop)	potraviny	pot-ra-vi-ni	šunka	ham	shoon-ka
ground floor	přízemí (P)	přzi-ze-**mee**	ruka (ruce)	hand(s)	roo-ka (roo-tse)
group (of people)	skupina	skoo-pi-na	kabelka	handbag	ka-bel-ka
guest (m/f)	host	host	kapesník	handkerchief	ka-pes-neek
guesthouse	penzion	pen-zi-yon	ruční práce	hand-made	rooch-**nee**
guide (m/f)	průvodce	**proo**-vod-tse	je to ruční	is it	ye to rooch-**nee**
	(průvodkyně)	(**proo**-vod-ki-ni̯e)	práce?	hand-made?	**pra**-tse?
guidebook	průvodce	proo-vod-tse	hands-free	hands-free	**pra**-tse
				(for phone)	
			stát se	to happen	stat se

English – Czech

English – Czech

what happened?	co se stalo?	tso se sta-lo?
happy	šťastný(-á/-é)	sht'ast-**nee** (-á/-**e**)
happy birthday!	všechno nejlepší k narozeninám!	**vshekh**-no ney-lep-**shee** k na-ro-ze-ni-**nam!**
Happy New Year!	šťastný Nový rok!	shť'ast-**nee** no-**vee** rok!
hard (tough)	tvrdý(-á/-é)	tvr-**dee**(-á/-**e**)
(of meat)	tuhý(-á/-é)	too-**hee**(-á/-**e**)
(difficult)	těžký(-á/-é)	t'yezh-**kee**(-**a**/-**e**)
to have	mít	meet; see GRAMMAR
he	on	on; see GRAMMAR
head	hlava	hla-va
headache	bolest hlavy	bo-lest hla-vi
I've got a headache	bolí mě hlava	bo-**lee** mnye hla-va
health noun	zdraví	zdra-**vee**
health-food shop	obchod se zdravou výživou	ob-khod se zdra-vow **vee**-zhi-vow
healthy adj	zdravý(-á/-é)	zdra-**vee**(-**a**/-**e**)
to hear	slyšet	sli-shet
heart	srdce	srrd-tse
to heat up (food)	ohřát	o-hřzat
heating	topení	to-pe-**nee**
heavy	těžký(-á/-é)	t'yezh-**kee**(-**a**/-**e**)
height	výška	veesh-ka
hello	dobrý den; ahoj	dob-**ree** den; a-hoy
help!	pomoc!	po-**motst!**
to help	pomáhat	po-**ma**-hat
can you help me?	můžete mi pomoct?	**moo**-zhe-te mi po-**motst?**
her	její	ye-**yee**
here	tady	ta-di
it's here	je tady	ye ta-di
it's not here	není to tady	ne-**nee** to ta-di

English	Czech	Pronunciation
here is her passport	tady je její pas	ta-dy-ye-ye-yee pas
hi!	ahoj!	a-hoy!
high	vysoký(-á/-é)	vi-so-**kee**(-**a**/-**e**)
him (with)	s ním	s neem
(about)	o něm	o nYem
(to)	k němu	k nYe-moo
hip	bok	bok
to hire	půjčit si	**pooy**-chit si
I want to hire a car	chci si půjčit auto	khtsi si **pooy**-chit aw-to
his	jeho	ye-ho
historic	historický (-á/-é)	his-to-rits-**kee** (-**a**/-**e**)
hobby	koníček	ko-**nee**-chek
to hold (contain)	obsahovat	ob-sa-ho-vat
hold-up noun (traffic)	zdržení	zdr-zhe-**nee**
holiday	svátek	**sva**-tek
	volný den	vol-**nee** den
I'm on holiday	mám dovolenou	mam do-vo-le-now
home	domov	do-mov
is he/she at home?	je doma?	ye-do-ma?
I'm going home	jdu domu	ydoo do-moo
homeopathic	homeopatický (-á/-é)	ho-me-o-pa-tits-**kee**-(-**a**/-**e**)
to hope	doufat	dow-fat
I hope so	doufám, že ano	dow-fam, zhe ano
I hope not	doufám, že ne	dow-fam, zhe ne
hors d'oeuvre	předkrm	pzhed-krrm
hospital	nemocnice	ne-mots-ni-tse
hot	horký(-á/-é); pálivý(-á/-é)	**pa**-li-**vee**(-**a**/-**e**);
I'm hot	je mi horko	ye mi hor-ko
it's too hot (room)	je tu příliš horko	ye too pzhee-lish hor-ko
hotel	hotel	ho-tel
hour	hodina	ho-di-na

English – Czech

English	Czech	Pronunciation
in an hour's time	za hodinu	za ho-di-noo
half an hour	půl hodina	pool ho-di-na
house	dům	doom
how	jak	yak
how much/ many?	kolik?	ko-lik?
how are you?	jak se máte?	yak se ma-te?
hungry: I'm hungry	mám hlad	mam hlad
hurry: I'm in a hurry	spěchám	spye-kham
hurt: it hurts	bolí to	bo-lee to
husband	manžel	man-zhel
I	já	ya: see GRAMMAR
ice	led	led
ice cream	zmrzlina	zmrr-zhli-na
ice lolly	nanuk	na-nook

Czech	English	Pronunciation
ledový(-á/-é)	*iced*	le-do-vee(:-a/-e)
nápad	*idea*	na-pad
jestliže	*if*	yest-li-zhe
nemocný (-á/-é)	*ill*	ne-mots-nee (-a/-e)
jsem nemocný	*I'm ill*	ysem ne-mots-nee
nemoc	*illness*	ne-mots
okamžitě	*immediately*	o-kam-zhi-t'ye
důležitý (-á/-é)	*important*	doo-le-zhi-tee (-a/-e)
je to nemožné	*impossible: it's impossible*	ye to ne-mozh-ne
v	*in*	v
před	*in front of*	přzhed
včetně	*included*	vchet-n'ye
nevýhodný (-á/-é)	*inconvenient*	ne-vee-hod-nee (-a/-e)
špatné trávení	*indigestion*	spat-ne tra-ve-nee
uvnitř	*indoors*	oov-nitzh

English	Czech	pronunciation
infection	infekce	in-fek-tse
informal	neformální	ne-for-mal-nee
information	informace	in-for-ma-tse
ingredients	přísady	přzhe-sa-di
to injure	zranit se	zra-nit-se
injured	poraněný (-á/-é)	po-ra-nye-nee (-a/-e)
insect	hmyz	hmiz
insect repellant	repelent	re-pe-lent
inside	uvnitř	oov-nitřzh
instant coffee	instantní káva	in-stant-nee ka-va
instead of (something)	místo (čeho)	mees-to
insurance	pojištění	po-yish-tye-nee
to insure	pojistit	po-yis-tit
insurance documents	doklady o pojištění	dok-la-dio po-yish-tye-nee
interesting	zajímavý (-á/-é)	za-yee-ma-vee (-a/-e)
international	mezinárodní	me-zi-na-rod-nee
into	do; dovnitř	do; dov-nitřzh
to introduce (someone to)	představit	přzhed-sta-vit
invitation	pozvání	poz-va-nee
to invite	pozvat	poz-vat
Ireland	Irsko	ir-sko
Irish (person) (m/f)	Ir(ka)	ir(ka)
adj	irský(-á/-é)	ir-skee
iron (metal) noun	železo	zhe-le-zo
iron (for clothes) noun	žehlička	zhe-hlich-ka
can I borrow an iron?	mohu si půjčit žehličku?	mo-hoo si pooy-chit? zhe-hlich-koo
to iron	žehlit	zhe-hlit
is	je	ye; see GRAMMAR
it	to	to; see GRAMMAR

English – Czech

itch: *it itches*	to svědí	to svYe-**dee**
Internet café	internetová kavárna	in-ter-ne-to-**va** ka-**var**-na
J		
jacket	sako; bunda	sa-ko; bun-da
jam (food)	džem,	dzhem,
	marmeláda	mar-me-**la**-da
jammed: *it's*	je to	ye to
jammed	zaseknuté	za-sek-noo-**te**
January	leden	le-den
jar (honey,	sklenice	skle-ni-tse
jam, etc.)		
jeans	džíny	dzhee-ni
jewellery	klenoty	kle-no-ti
Jewish adj	židovský	zhi-dov-**skee**
	(-á/-é)	(-**a**/-**e**)
job	práce	pra-tse
what's your	jaké je vaše	ya-**kee** ye va-she
job?	povolání?	po-vo-**la**-nee?
joint	kloub	klowb
journey	cesta	tses-ta
juice	džus	dzhoos
July	červenec	cher-ve-nets
June	červen	cher-ven
just (just two)	jen dvě	yen dvYe
I've just	právě jsem	pra-vYe ysem
arrived	přijel	přzhi-yel
K		
to keep	držet;	dr-zhet;
	nechat si	ne-khat si
keep the	nechte si	nekh-te si
change	drobné	drob-**nee**
key	klíč	kleech
kidneys	ledviny	led-vi-ni
kilo	kilo	ki-lo
kilogram	kilogram	ki-lo-gram
kilometre	kilometr	ki-lo-me-tr
kind	laskavý(-á/-é)	las-ka-**vee**(-**a**/-**e**)
you're very	jste velmi	yste vel-mi
kind	laskavý(-á)	las-ka-**vee**(-**a**)
knee	koleno	ko-le-no

English	Czech	Pronunciation
to knock (on door)	zaklepat	zak-le-pat
to know	vědět; znát	vye-dYet; znat
I know	vím; znám	veem; znam
I don't know	nevím; neznám	ne-veem; nez-nam
I know how to swim	umím plavat	oo-meem pla-vat
L		
ladies (toilet)	Dámy; ženy	da-mi; zhe-ni
lamb (meat)	jehněčí	ye-hnYe-chee
lamp	lampa	lam-pa
land: has the plane landed?	už to letadlo přistálo?	oozh to le-tad-lo pРzhi-sta-lo?
language	jazyk	ya-zik
large	velký(-á/-é);	vel-kee(-a/-e);
last	poslední; minulý(-á/-é)	pos-led-nee; mi-noo-lee (-a/-e)
last week	minulý týden	mi-noo-lee tee-den
the last train	poslední vlak	pos-led-nee vlak
late	pozdě	poz-dYe
the train is late	vlak má zpoždění	vlak ma zpozh-dYe-nee
sorry I'm late	promiňte, že jdu pozdě	pro-minY-te, zhe y-doo poz-dYe
later	později	poz-dYe-yi
to laugh	smát se	smat se
laxative	záchod	za-khod
to learn (study) (information)	projímadlo naučit se dozvědět se	pro-Yee-mad-lo na-oo-chit se doz-vYe-dYet se
leather	kůže	koo-zhe
leave (on foot) (in vehicle)	odejít odjet	o-de-yeet od-yet
when does the bus leave?	kdy odjíždí ten autobus?	kdi od-yeezh-dee ten aW-to-boos?
left	levý(-á/-é)	le-vee(-a/-e)
on/to the left	vlevo	vle-vo

English – Czech

English	Czech	Pronunciation
left-luggage office	úschovna zavazadel	**oos**-khow-na za-va-za-del
leg	noha	no-ha
lemon	citrón	tsit-**ron**
lemonade	limonáda	li-mo-**na**-da
to lend	půjčit	**pooy**-chit
length	délka	**del**-ka
lens (for camera)	objektiv	ob-**yek**-tiv
(contact lens)	kontaktní čočky	kon-takt-**nee** choch-ki
less	méně	me-**nye**
(less than)	méně než	me-**nye** nezh
to let (allow)	dovolit	do-vo-lit
letter (mail)	dopis	do-pis
licence (driving)	řidičský průkaz	**zhi**-dich-s**kee** **proo**-kaz
lift (elevator)	výtah	**vee**-tah
light adj (not heavy)	lehký(-á/-é)	leh-**kee**(-**a**/-**e**)
(of colour)	světlý(-á/-é)	svYet-**lee**(-**a**/-**e**)
light noun (illumination)	světlo	svYet-lo
car lights	světla	svYet-la
like prep	jako	ya-ko
I want one	chci takový	khtsi ta-ko-**vee**
like this	jako tento	ya-ko-ten-to
to like	mít rád(a)	meet **rad**(a)
I like coffee	mám rád(a) kávu	mám **rad**(a) ka-voo
I don't like...	nemám rád(a) kávu	ne-mám **rad**(a) ka-voo
I'd like...	chtěl(a) bych...	khtYel(a) bikh...
coffee	káva	rzha-da
line (queue, row)	řada	lin-ka
(telephone)	linka	ye-le-**nee looy**
lip salve	jelení lůj	li-**ker**
liqueur	likér	sez-nam
list	seznam	pos-**low**-khat
listen (to)	poslouchat	li-tr
litre	litr	ma-**lee**(-**a**/-**e**), ma-lo
little (small)	malý(-á/-é), málo	

English	Czech	Pronunciation
just a little, please	jenom trochu, prosím	yᵉ-nom tro-**khoo**, pro-**seem**
litter	odpadky	od-**pad**-ki
liver	játra	**yat**-ra
to live	žít; bydlet	zheet; **bid**-let
I live in London	bydlím v Londýně	**bid**-leem v lon-**dee**-nʸe
local	místní	**meest**-nee
to lock	zamknout	zam-**knowt**
London	Londýn	lon-**deen**
long	dlouhý(-á/-é)	dlowʰ-**hee**(-**a**/-**e**)
will it take long?	bude to trvat dlouho?	**boo**-de to tr-**vat** **dlow**-ho?
look at	dívat se	**dee**-vat se
look after	starat se	**sta**-rat se
look for	hledat	**hle**-dat
lose	ztratit	**ztra**-tit
lost	ztracený (-á/-é)	ztra-tse-**nee** (-**a**/-**e**)
I've lost my wallet	ztratil(a) jsem peněženku	ztra-til ysem pe-nʸe-**zhen**-koo

English	Czech	Pronunciation
I'm lost	zabloudil(a) jsem	zab-lowʰ-**dil**(a) ysem
lost property office	ztráty a nálezy	**ztra**-ti a **na**-le-zi
lot: *a lot*	mnoho	**mno**-ho
loud	hlasitý(-á/-é)	hla-si-**tee**(-**a**/-**e**)
lounge (in hotel, airport)	hala	**ha**-la
love noun	láska	**las**-ka
to love (to enjoy)	milovat	**mi**-lo-vat
I love cheese	mám rád(a) sýr	mam **ra**-d(a) seer
I love you	miluji tě	mee-**loo**-yee tě
lovely: *it's lovely*	to je pěkně	to ye **pʸek**-ne
low (standard, quality)	nízký(-a/-e)	**neez**-kee(-**a**/-**e**)
low-fat adj	nízkotučný (-á/-é)	neez-ko-**tooch**-nee(-**a**/-**e**)
to lower the volume	snížit hlasitost	**snee**-zhit hla-si-tost

English – Czech

English – Czech

English	Czech	Pronunciation
luck	štěstí	shtYes-**tee**
lucky: *I'm lucky*	mám štěstí	mam shtYes-**tee**
luggage	zavazadlo	za-va-zad-lo
luggage trolley	vozík	vo-**zeek**
lunch	oběd	o-bYed
M		
mad (angry)	rozzlobený (-**á/-é**)	roz-lo-be-**nee** (-**a/-e**)
magazine	časopis	cha-so-pis
maid	pokojská	po-koy-ska
mail	pošta	posh-ta
main	hlavní	hlav-**nee**
main course	hlavní chod	hlav-**nee** khod
to make	dělat, vyrábět	dYe-lat, vi-ra-bYet
make-up	make-up	
male	muž	moozh
man	muž	moozh
(generally)	člověk	chlo-vYek

English	Czech	Pronunciation
to manage (to direct)	řídit	rzhee-dit
manager	manažer; vedoucí	ma-na-zher; ve-dow-tsee
many	mnoho	mno-ho
how many?	kolik?	ko-lik?
map	mapa	ma-pa
March	březen	bRzhe-zen
marmalade	pomerančový džem	po-me-ran-cho-vee dzhem
married (man)	ženatý	zhe-na-**tee**
married (woman)	vdaná	vda-na
I'm married	jsem ženatý (vdaná)	ysem zhe-na-tee (vda-na)
are you married?	jste ženatý (vdaná)?	yste zhe-na-tee (vda-na)?
to marry	oženit se, vdát se	o-zhe-nit se, vdat se
material (cloth)	látka	lat-ka
matter: *it doesn't matter*	to nevadí	to ne-va-dee

English	Czech	Pronunciation
May	květen	kvYe-ten
me	mě, mnou	mnYe, mnoW
meal	jídlo	yeed-lo
to mean (signify)	znamenat	zna-me-nat
what does this mean?	co to znamená?	tso to zna-me-ná?
meat	maso	ma-so
medicine	lék	lek
medium: medium-sized	středně velký	stŽhed-nYe vel-kee
to meet	potkat; setkat se s	pot-kat; set-kat se s
pleased to meet you	těší mě	tYe-shee mnYe
memory	paměť	pa-mnYetY
men	muži	moo-zhi
to mend	opravit	o-pra-vit
menu	jídelní lístek	yee-del-nee lees-tek
message	vzkaz	vzkaz
can I leave a message?	mohu nechat vzkaz?	mo-hoo ne-khat vzkaz?
metre	metr	metr
metro (underground)	metro	met-ro
midnight	půlnoc	pool-nots
mild	mírný(-á/-é)	meer-nee(-a/-e)
milk	mléko	mle-ko
with/without milk	s mlékem / bez mléka	s mle-kem / bez mle-ka
mind: do you mind if I smoke?	Nevadí Vám když si zapálím?	ne-va-dee vam kdizh si za-pa-leem?
I don't mind	nevadí mi	ne-va-dee mi
mineral water	minerálka	mi-ne-ral-ka
minute	minuta	mi-noo-ta
to miss (plane, train, etc.)	zmeškat	zmesh-kat
Miss	slečna	slech-na
missing: my... is missing	ztratil(a) se mi...	ztra-til(a) se mi...

English – Czech

English	Czech	Pronunciation
mistake	chyba	khi-ba
misunderstanding	nedorozumění	ne-do-ro-zoo-mnYe-nee
modern	moderní	mo-der-nee
Monday	pondělí	pon-dYe-lee
money	peníze	pe-nee-ze
I've lost my money	ztratil(a) jsem peníze	ztra-ti-l(a) ysem pe-nee-ze
month	měsíc	mnYe-seets
this month	tento měsíc	ten-to mnYe-seets
last month	minulý měsíc	mi-noo-lee mnYe-seets
next month	příští měsíc	pZheesh-tee mnYe-seets
more	víc	veets
I've no more money	už nemám peníze	oozh ne-mam pe-nee-ze
more bread, please	ještě chleba, prosím	yesh-tYe khle-ba pro-seem
can I have	mohu dostat	mo-hoo dos-tat
some more?	víc?	veets?
morning	ráno	ra-no
most	většina, nejvíce	vYet-shi-na, ney-vee-tse
mother	máma, matka	ma-ma, mat-ka
motor	motor	mo-tor
motorboat	motorový člun	mo-to-ro-vee chloon
motorway	dálnice	dal-ni-tse
mouth	ústa	oos-ta
to move	pohybovat	po-hi-bo-vat
Mr	pan	pan
Mrs	paní	pa-nee
much	mnoho	mno-ho
too much	příliš mnoho	pZhee-lish mno-ho
mugging	přepadení	pZhe-pa-de-nee
muscle	sval	sval
I've pulled a muscle	natáhl(a) jsem si sval	na-ta-hl(a) ysem si sval
museum	muzeum	moo-ze-oom

English	Czech	Pronunciation
mushrooms	houby	hoW-bi
music	hudba	hood-ba
must: *I must go*	musím jít	moos-e)em yeet
we must go	musíme jít	moos-see-me yeet
you mustn't	nesmíš	nes-meesh
my (m/f/nt)	můj/moje/	mooy/mo-ye/
	moje	mo-ye
my passport	můj pas	mooy pas

N

English	Czech	Pronunciation
name	jméno	yme-no
my name is...	jmenuji se...	yme-noo-yi se...
what's your name?	jak se jmenujete?	yak se yme-noo-ye-te?
narrow	úzký(-á/-é)	ooz-kee(-a/-e)
national	národní	na-rod-nee
nationality	národnost	na-rod-nost
nature	příroda	p'zhee-ro-da
natural	přírodní	p'zhee-rod-nee
near	blízko	bleez-ko

English	Czech	Pronunciation
is it near?	je to blízko?	ye to bleez-ko?
near the bank	blízko banky	bleez-ko ban-ki
where's the	kde je	ney-blizh-shee
nearest	nejbližší	we-blizh-shee
chemist?	lékárna?	le-kar-na?
necessary	nutný(-á/-é)	noot-nee(-a/-e)
neck	krk	krk
to need	potřebovat	pot-rzhe-bo-vat
I need...	potřebuji...	pot-rzhe-boo-yi...
we need to go	potřebujeme	pot-rzhe-boo-ye-
	jet	me yet
never	nikdy	nik-di
I never eat	nikdy nejím	nik-di ne-yeem
meat	maso	ma-so
new	nový(-á/-é)	no-vee(-a/-e)
news	zprávy	zpra-vi
newspaper	noviny	no-vi-ni
newsstand	novinový	novi-no-vee
	stánek	sta-nek
New Year	Nový rok	no-vee rok

English – Czech

English	Czech	Pronunciation
New Zealand	Nový Zéland	no-vee ze-land
next	příští	pzheesh-tee
when is the next bus?	kdy jede příští autobus?	kdi ye-de pzheesh-tee aw-to-boos?
next to	vedle	ved-le
nice (friendly)	pěkný(-á/-é)	pyek-nee(-a/-e)
	sympatický	sim-pa-tits-kee(-a/-e)
night	noc	nots
last night	včera v noci	vchera v no-tsi
no	ne	ne
no, thanks	ne, děkuji	ne, dye-koo-yi
there's no hot water	neteče teplá voda	ne-te-che tep-la vo-da
nobody	nikdo	nik-do
noise	hluk	hlook
noisy	hlučný(-á/-é)	hlooch-nee(-á/-e)
non-alcoholic	nealkoholický(-á/-é)	ne-al-ko-ho-lits-kee(-á/-é)
none	žádný(-á/-é)	zhad-nee(-á/-é)
north	sever	se-ver
Northern Ireland	Severní Irsko	se-ver-nee ir-sko
not	ne	ne
I don't know	nevím	ne-veem
nothing	nic	nits
nothing else	nic jiného	nits yi-ne-ho
notice	oznámení	oz-na-me-nee
November	listopad	lis-to-pad
now	nyní; teď	ni-nee; te
nowhere	nikde	nik-de
number	číslo	chees-lo

O

English	Czech	Pronunciation
to obtain	dostat	dos-tat
October	říjen	rzhee-yen
of	z	z
a glass of beer	sklenice piva	skle-ni-tse pi-va
made of	vyrobeno z	vi-ro-be-no z

English	Czech	Pronunciation
off: *the heating is off*	topení je vypnuté	to-pe-**nee** ye vip-noo-**te**
this is off (milk, food)	je to zkažené	ye to zka-zhe-**ne**
office	kancelář	kan-tse-**la**zh
often	často	**chas**-to
how often?	jak často?	yak **chas**-to?
OK	dobře	dob-**rzhe**
old	starý(-á/-é)	sta-**ree**(-**a**/-**e**)
how old are you?	kolik je vám roků?	**ko**-lik je **vam** ro-**koo**?
I'm ... years old	je mi ... roků	ye mi...ro-**koo**
how old is it?	jak je to staré?	yak ye to sta-**re**?
on	v; na	v; na
once	jednou	yed-**now**
at once	okamžitě	o-kam-zhi-**t**ye
one (m/f/nt)	jeden/jedna/jedno	**ye**-den/yed-na/yed-no
only	jenom	**ye**-nom
open adj	otevřený(-á/-é)	o-tev-**rzhe**-nee(-**a**/-**e**)
to open	otevřít	o-tev-**rzheet**
what time does it open?	v kolik hodin se otevírá?	v ko-lik ho-din se o-te-**vee-ra?**
opposite	naproti	na-pro-ti
or	nebo	ne-bo
orange adj	oranžový (-á/-é)	o-ran-zho-**vee** (-**a**/-**e**)
orange noun	pomeranč	po-me-ranch
order noun	pořádek	po-**zha**-dek
out of order (food)	nefunguje	ne-foon-goo-ye
to order	objednat	ob-yed-nat
to organize	organizovat	or-ga-ni-zo-vat
other	jiný	**yee**-nee
our (m/f/nt)	náš/naše/naše	**nash**/na-she/na-she
out	ven	ven
he's gone out	je venku; odešel	ye ven-koo; o-de-shel
over	přes	pzhes
overcast	zataženo	za-ta-zhe-no
to overcharge	předražit	pzhe-dra-zhit

English – Czech

English – Czech

English	Czech	Pronunciation
P		
to pack	balit	ba-lit
package (parcel)	balíček	ba-**lee**-chek
package tour	zájezd	**za**-yezd
packet	balíček; sáček	ba-**lee**-chek; **sa**-chek
paid: *I've paid already*	už jsem platil(a)	oozh ysem pla-**til**(a)
pain	bolest	**bo**-lest
painful	bolestivý (-á/-é)	bo-les-ti-**vee** (-**a**/-**é**)
painkillers	léky proti bolesti	**le**-ki pro-ti **bo**-les-ti
painting (picture)	obraz	**ob**-raz
pair	pár	par
pale	bledý(-á/-é)	ble-**dee**(-**a**/-**é**)
pants (underpants)	slipy	**sli**-pi
paper	papír	pa-**peer**
parcel	balík	ba-**leek**
pardon?	prosím	pro-**seem** ne-
I beg your pardon?	nerozumím prosím?	ro-zoo-**meem** pro-**seem?**
parents	rodiče	**ro**-di-che
park noun	park	park
to park	parkovat	par-ko-vat
part	část	chast
spare part	náhradní díl	**na**-hrad-nee **deel**
partner (business)(m/f)	partner(ka)	part-ner(-ka)
my partner (m/f)	můj přítel/ moje přítelkyně	**mooy** **pzhee**-tel/ mo-ye **pzhee**-tel-ki-nYe
party (celebration)	večírek	ve-**chee**-rek
passenger (m/f)	cestující	tses-too-**yee**-tsee
passport	pas	pas

English	Czech	Pronunciation		English	Czech	Pronunciation
pasta	těstoviny	t'yes-to-vi-ni		**per**	na; za	na; za
pastry (dough)	těsto	t'yes-to		*per hour*	za hodinu	za ho-di-noo
path (in mountains)	cesta	tses-ta		*per person*	na osobu	na o-so-boo
	stezka	stez-ka		**perfect**	perfektní	per-fekt-nee
to pay	platit	pla-tit		**performance**	představení	pzhed-sta-ve-nee
where do I pay?	kde se platí?	kde se pla-tee?		**perhaps**	možná	mozh-na
payment	platba	plat-ba		**person**	osoba	o-so-ba
peace	klid, mír	klid, meer		**petrol**	benzín	ben-zin
peanut allergy	alergie na burské oříšky	a-ler-gi-ye na boor-skee o-zheesh-ki		**pharmacy**	lékárna	le-kar-na
				to phone	telefonovat	te-le-fo-no-vat
pears	hrušky	hroosh-ky		*see telephone*		
peas	hrášky	hrash-ky		*by phone*	telefonem	te-le-fo-nem
to peel	oloupat	o-low-pat		**phonecard**	telefonní karta	te-le-fo-nee kar-ta
pen	pero	pe-ro		**photocopy** noun	kopie	ko-pi-ye
pensioner (m/f)	důchodce (důchodkyně)	doo-khod-tse (doo-khod-ki-nYe)		**to photocopy**	kopírovat	ko-pee-ro-vat
				photograph noun	fotograf	fo-to-graf
people	lidé	li-de		*to take a photo*	vyfotit	vi-fo-tit
pepper (spice)	pepř	pepzh		**phrasebook**	konverzační příručka	kon-ver-zach-nee pzhee-rooch-ka
pepper (vegetable)	paprika	pap-ri-ka				

English – Czech

English	Czech	pronunciation
to pick (fruit, flowers)	sbírat, trhat	sbee-rat, tr-hat
(to choose)	vybrat	vib-rat
piece	kousek	koW-sek
pillow	polštář	polsh-**ta**'zh
Pilsen	Plzeň	pl-zenY
pink	růžový(-á/-é)	**roo**-zho-**vee** (-**a**/-e)
pity: what a pity!	to je škoda!	to ye shko-da!
place	místo	mees-to
place of birth	místo narození	mees-to na-ro-ze-**nee**
plain (unflavoured)	bez příchuti	bez pr̆hee-khoo-ti
plane (aeroplane)	letadlo	le-tad-lo
plasters	náplasti	na-plas-ti
plastic	z umělé hmoty	zoo-mnYe-**le** hmo-ti

English	Czech	pronunciation
platform (railway)	nástupiště	nas-too-pish-t̆Ye
from which platform?	z jakého nástupiště?	z ya-ke-ho nas-too-pish-t̆Ye?
play noun (theatre)	hra	hra
to play (theatre, game)	hrát	hrat
pleasant	příjemný (-á/-é)	pr̆zhee-yem-nee (-**a**/-e)
please	prosím	pro-**seem**
plums	švestky	shvest-ki
plum jam	povidla	po-vid-la
pocket	kapsa	kap-sa
point	bod	bod
poisonous	jedovatý (-á/-é)	ye-do-va-**tee** (-**a**/-e)
police	policie	po-li-tsi-ye
police station	policejní stanice	po-li-tsey-nee sta-ni-tse
poor (not rich)	chudý(-á/-é)	khoo-**dee** (-**a**/-e)

English	Czech	Pronunciation
pork	vepřové	vep-ʐho-**ve**
porter (for door)	vrátný	vrat-**nee**
(for luggage)	nosič	no-sich
possible	možný(-á/-é)	mozh-**nee**(-**a**/-**e**)
is it possible to...?	je možné...?	ye mozh-**ne**?
post: by post	poštou	posh-tow
to post	poslat	pos-lat
postbox	poštovní schránka	posh-tov-**nee** skhran-ka
postcard	pohled	po-hled
postcode	poštovní směrovací číslo	posh-tov-**nee** smn-ʸe-ro-va-tsee chee-slo
post office	pošta	posh-ta
potato	brambora	bram-bo-ra
pound (weight) = approx. 0.5 kilo	libra	lib-ra
Prague	Praha	pra-ha
power (electricity)	elektřina	e-lekt-ʐhi-na
to prefer	dávat přednost	**da**-vat pʐhed-nost
to prepare	připravovat	pʐhi-pra-vo-vat
prescription	předpis	pʐhed-pis
present (gift)	dárek	**da**-rek
pretty	hezký(-á/-é)	hez-**kee**(-**a**/-**e**)
price	cena	tse-na
price list	seznam cen	sez-nam tsen
private	soukromý (-á/-é)	sow-kro-**nee** (-**a**/-**e**)
probably	asi	a-si
problem	problém (-á/-é)	prob-lem
prohibited	zakázaný (-á/-é)	za-ka-za-**nee** (-**a**/-**e**)
promise noun	slib	slib
to promise	slíbit	slee-bit
to pronounce	vyslovovat	vis-lo-vo-vat
how is this pronounced?	jak se tohle vyslovuje?	yak se to-hle vis-lo-voo-ye?
prunes	sušené švestky	soo-she-**ne** shvest-ki

to provide	zařídit	za-**zhee**-dit	quiet	tichý(-á/-é)	ti-**khee**(-a/-e)
public	veřejný(-á/-é)	ve-**zhey**-nee (-a/-e)	*I want a*	chci pokoj	khtsi ti-**khee**
			quiet room		
public holiday	státní svátek	**stat**-nee sva-tek	quiet!	ticho!	**ti**-kho!
pudding	zákusek	**za**-koo-sek	quite	docela	do-tse-la
to pull	táhnout	**ta**-hnowt	*it's quite good*	je to docela dobré	ye to do-tse-la dob-**re**
puncture	defekt	de-**fekt**			
purse	peněženka	pe-**nYe**-zhen-ka	**R**		
I've lost my	z tratil(a) jsem	ztra-til(a) ysem	race (sport)	závod	**za**-vod
purse	peněženku	pe-**nYe**-zhen-koo	radio	rádio	**ra**-di-yo
to push	tlačit	tla-chit	railway station	nádraží	nad-ra-**zhee**
to put (to place)	položit	po-lo-zhit	rain noun	déšt'	deshtY
			to rain	pršet	pr-shet
Q			raining: *it's*	prší	pr-**shee**
			raining		
quality	kvalita	kva-li-ta	raped	znásilněná	zna-sil-nYe-**na**
quantity	množství	mnozh-**stvee**	rare (steak)	málo	**ma**-lo
quarter	čtvrt	chtvrtY		propečený	pro-pe-che-**nee**
question noun	otázka	o-**taz**-ka	(unique)	vzácný	**vzats**-nee
queue	fronta	fron-ta	rash (skin)	vyrážka	vi-**razh**-ka
quick	rychlý(-á/-é)	ri-khlee(-a/-e)	rate	kurs	koors
quickly	rychle	ri-khle			

English	Czech	Pronunciation
what's the exchange rate?	jaký je kurs?	**ya**-kee ye koors?
raw	syrový(-á/-é)	si-ro-**vee**(-**a**/-**e**)
razor blades	žiletky	zhi-**let**-ki
to read	číst	cheest
ready	hotový(-á/-é)	ho-to-**vee**(-**a**/-**e**)
is it ready?	je to hotové?	ye ho-to-**ve**?
to get ready	připravit se	přzhi-**pra**-vit se
real (genuine)	pravý(-á/-é)	pra-**vee**(-**a**/-**e**)
receipt	potvrzení	pot-vr-ze-**nee**
reception	recepce	re-**tsep**-tse
recommend	doporučit	do-po-roo-**chit**
what do you recommend?	co doporučujete?	tso do-po-roo-**choo**-ye-te?
red	červený(-á/-é)	**cher**-ve-**nee** (-**a**/-**e**)
to reduce (price)	slevnit	**slev**-nit
reduction	sleva	**sle**-va
is there a reduction?	poskytujete slevu?	pos-ki-**too**-ye-te **sle**-voo?
refill (for gas cylinder, etc.)	náhradní náplň	na-hrad-**nee** na-**plnY**
refund	finanční náhrada	fi-**nan**-chnee na-**hra**-da
to refuse	odmítnout	od-**meet**-noWt
regarding	týkající se	tee-ka-**yee**-tsee se
relationship	příbuzenský vztah	přzhee-boo-zen-**skee** vztah
to remember	pamatovat si	pa-ma-to-vat si
I don't remember	nevzpomínám si	nev-zpo-**mee**-nam si
to remove	odstranit	od-**stra**-nit
to rent	pronajmout si	pro-nay-**moWt** si
to repair	opravit	o-**pra**-vit
can you repair this?	můžete to opravit?	**moo**-zhe-te to o-**pra**-vit?
to repeat	opakovat	o-**pa**-ko-vat
to reply	odpovědět	od-po-**vye**-dyet
report noun	zpráva	**zpra**-va
request	žádost	**zha**-dost

English – Czech

reservation	rezervace	re-zer-va-tse	
I have a reservation	mám rezervaci	mam re-zer-va-tsi	
to reserve (room, table, etc.)	rezervovat si	re-zer-vo-vat si	
to rest	odpočinout si	od-po-chi-noWts si	
restaurant	restaurace	res-taW-ra-tse	
retired	v důchodu	v doo-kho-doo	
I'm retired	jsem v důchodu	ysem v doo-kho-doo	
to return (come back)	vrátit se	vra-tit se	
(give back)	vrátit	vra-tit	
return ticket	zpáteční jízdenka	zpa-tech-nee yeez-den-ka	
rice	rýže	ree-zhe	
rich (person)	bohatý(-á/-é)	bo-ha-tee(-a/-e)	
right (not left)	pravý(-á/-é)	pra-vee(-a/-e)	
on/to the right	vpravo	pra-vo	
right (correct)	správný(-á/-é)	sprav-nee(-a/-e)	
to ring (bell)	zvonit	zvo-nit	

ring road	dopravní okruh	do-prav-nee ok-rooh	
river	řeka	řzhe-ka	
road	silnice	sil-ni-tse	
road map	autoatlas	aW-to at-las	
road sign	dopravní značka	dop-rav-nee znach-ka	
roll (bread)	rohlík	ro-hleek	
Romany (person) (m/f)	Rom(-ka)	rom(-ka)	
adj	romský(-á/-é)	rom-skee(-a/-e)	
room (in house, etc.)	pokoj	po-koy	
(space)	prostor	pros-tor	
room service	pokojová obsluha	po-ko-yo-va ob-sloo-ha	
round (in theatre, etc.)	kulatý(-á/-é)	koo-la-tee(-a/-e)	
roundabout	kruhový objezd	kroo-ho-vee ob-yezd	
row (in theatre, etc.)	řada	řzha-da	

English	Czech	pronunciation			
rowing boat	člun	chloon	sanitary pads	menstruační	men-stroo-ach-
rubbish	odpadky	od-pad-ki		vložky	nee vlozh-ki
to run	běžet	bye-zhet	Saturday	sobota	so-bo-ta
			sauce	omáčka	o-mach-ka
S			sauerkraut	kyselé zelí	ki-sele ze-lee
			sausage	uzenina	oo-ze-ni-na
safe noun (for	sejf	seyf	savoury adj	slaný(-á/-é)	sla-nee(-**a/-e**)
valuables)			is it savoury	je to slané	ye to sla-ne
safe adj	bezpečný	bez-pech-nee	or sweet?	nebo sladké?	ne-bo slad-ke?
	(-á/-é)	(-**a/-e**)	to say	říkat	rzhee-kat
is it safe?	je to	ye to	school	škola	shko-la
	bezpečné?	bez-pech-ne?	Scotland	Skotsko	skot-sko
salad	salát	sa-lat	Scottish adj	skotský(-á/-é)	skot-skee(-**a/-e**)
mixed salad	míchaný salát	mee-kha-nee	sculpture	socha	so-kha
		sa-lat	to search	hledat	hle-dat
salami	salám	sa-lam	season (of year)	roční období	roch-nee
sales	slevy	sle-vi			ob-do-bee
salt	sůl	sool	seasoning	koření	ko-rzhe-nee
same: *the*	to samé	to sa-me	season ticket	permanentka	per-ma-nent-ka
same			seat (chair) (on	židle	zhid-le
sandwich	sendvič	send-vich	bus, train, etc.)	sedadlo	se-dad-lo

English – Czech

English	Czech	Pronunciation
seatbelt	bezpečnostní pás	bez-pech-nost-nee pas
second adj	druhý(-á/-é)	droo-hee(-a/-é)
second-class	druhá třída	droo-ha t'zhee-da
a second-class ticket	jízdenka druhé třídy	yeez-den-ka droo-he t'zhee-di
to see	vidět	vi-dyet
to sell	prodávat	pro-da-vat
do you sell...?	prodáváte...?	pro-da-va-te?
to send	posílat	po-see-lat
separate	oddělený(-á/-é)	od-dye-le-nee
we'd like	chtěli bychom	kht'ye-li bi-khom
separate beds	oddělené postele	od-dye-le-ne pos-te-le
September	září	za-rzhee
serious: is it serious?	je to vážně?	ye to vazh-ne?
service	obsluha	ob-sloo-ha
shade (shadow)	stín	steen
in the shade	ve stínu	ve stee-noo
to shake (bottle)	protřepat	pro-t'zhe-pat
sharp (razor, blade)	ostrý(-á/-é)	os-tree(-a/-é)
to shave	holit	ho-lit
she	ona	o-na; see GRAMMAR
sheet (for bed)	prostěradlo	pros-tye-rad-lo
shirt	košile	ko-shi-le
shoe	bota	bo-ta
shop	obchod	ob-khod
shop assistant (m/f)	prodavač(ka)	pro-da-vach(-ka)
shopping	nakupování	na-koo-po-va-nee
(items bought)	nákupy	na-koo-pi
short	krátký(-á/-é)	krat-kee(-a/-é)
short-cut	zkratka	zkrat-ka
is there a short-cut?	je tu zkratka?	ye too zkrat-ka?

English	Czech	Pronunciation
shorts (short trousers)	šortky	short-ki
shoulder	rameno	ra-me-no
show noun (entertainment)	představení	pʳzhed-sta-ve-nee
to show *please show me*	ukázat prosím, ukažte mi	oo-ka-zat pro-seem, oo-kazh-te mi
shower	sprcha	sprr-kha
shut adj	zavřený(-á/-é)	zav-ʳzhe-nee (-a/-e)
to shut (close)	zavírat	za-vee-rat
sick: *I feel sick*	je mi špatně	ye mi shpat-nYe
side	strana	stra-na
sightseeing	prohlídka památihodností	pro-hleed-ka pa-mYe-ti-hod-nos-tee
sign noun (road-, notice, etc.)	značka	znach-ka
to sign (cheque, etc.)	označit	o-zna-chit
signature	podpis	pod-pis
silver	stříbro	stʳzheeb-ro
similar	podobný (-á/-é)	po-dob-nee (-a/-e)
since (time)	od	od
single: *I'm single*	jsem svobodný(-á)	ysem svo-bod-nee(-a)
single ticket	jízdenka tam	yeez-den-ka tam
sir (spoken form of address)	pán pane	pa-ne pa-ne
sister	sestra	ses-tra
to sit	sedět	se-dYet
please, sit down	posaďte se prosím	po-sadY-te se pro-seem
size (clothes) (shoes)	velikost číslo	ve-li-kost chees-lo
to ski	lyžovat	li-zho-vat
ski lift	lyžařský vlek	li-zhaʳzh-skee vlek
ski pass	permanentka	per-ma-nent-ka
skis	lyže	li-zhe

English – Czech

English	Czech	Pronunciation
skin	kůže	koo-zhe
skirt	sukně	sook-nYe
to sleep	spát	spat
slice	plátek	pla-tek
Slovak adj	slovenský (-á/-é)	slo-ven-skee (-á/-e)
I don't speak	nemluvím	ne-mloo-veem
Slovak	slovensky	slo-ven-ski
Slovakia	Slovensko	slo-ven-sko
slow	pomalý(-á/-é)	po-ma-lee(-a/-e)
slowly	pomalu	po-ma-loo
small	malý(-á/-é)	ma-lee(-a/-e)
smell noun	vůně	voo-nYe
to smell (good)	vonět	vo-nYet
(bad)	smrdět	smr-dYet
smile noun	úsměv	oos-mnYev
smoke noun	kouř	koWzh
to smoke	kouřit	koW-zhit
can I smoke here?	mohu tady kouřit?	mo-hoo ta-di koW-zhit?
smoked (meat, fish, cheese)	uzený(-á/-é)	oo-ze-nee(-á/-é)
snow	sníh	sneeh
to snow	sněžit	snYe-zhit
so	tak	tak
soap	mýdlo	meed-lo
sofa	gauč	gaWch
soft	měkký(-á/-é)	mnYe-kee(-a/-e)
some	nějaký(-á/-é)	nYe-ya-kee (-a/-e)
a few	několik	nYe-ko-lik
someone	někdo	nYek-do
something	něco	nYe-tso
sometimes	někdy	nYek-di
somewhere	někde	nYek-de
son	syn	sin
song	píseň	pee-senY
soon	brzy	br-zi
as soon as possible	co nejdříve	tso ney-dzhee-ve

English	Czech	Pronunciation
sore throat	bolení v krku	bo-le-nee v krr-koo
sorry!	promiňte!	pro-miny-te!
soup	polévka	po-lev-ka
sour	kyselý(-á/-é)	ki-se-lee(-a/-e)
south	jih	yih
spa	lázně	laz-nye
sparkling	perlivý(-á/-é)	per-li-vee(-a/-e)
to speak	mluvit	mloo-vit
	mluvíte	mloo-vee-te
do you speak English?	anglicky?	ang-glits-ki?
special	zvláštní	zvlasht-nee
speciality	specialita	spe-tsi-a-li-ta
speed	rychlost	rikh-lost
speed limit	omezení rychlosti	o-me-ze-nee rikh-los-ti
spell: how do you spell it?	jak se to hláskuje?	yak se to hlas-koo-ye?
to spend (of money)	utratit	oo-tra-tit
(of time)	trávit	tra-vit
spicy	pikantní(-á/-é)	pi-kant-nee (-a/-e)
to spill	rozlít	roz-leet
spirits (alcohol)	lihoviny	li-ho-vi-ni
spoon	lžíce	lzhee-tse
sport	sport	sport
spot (stain)	skvrna	skvr-na
(place)	místo	mees-to
spring (season)	jaro	ya-ro
square (in town)	náměstí	na-mnyes-tee
stadium	stadion	sta-di-yon
staff	zaměstnanci	za-mnyest-nan-tsi
stairs	schody	skho-di
stamp	známka	znam-ka
to stand	stát	stat
star	hvězda	hvyez-da
to start	začít	za-cheet
starter (in meal)	předkrm	przhed-krm
station	nádraží	nad-ra-zhee
statue	socha	so-kha

English – Czech

English – Czech

English	Czech	Pronunciation
to stay	být ubytovaný	oo-bi-to-va-nee
I'm staying at the... Hotel	jsem ubytovaný v hotelu...	ysem / v ho-te-loo...
to steal	krást	krast
steep: is it steep?	je to prudke?	ye to prood-ke?
step (stair)	schod	skhod
still (not fizzy)	neperlivý (-á/-é)	ne-per-li-vee
stolen	ukradený (-á/-é)	oo-kra-de-nee
stomach ache	bolesti břicha	bo-les-ti b'zhi-kha
stop!	stop!	stop!
store	obchod	ob-khod
straight on	rovně	rov-nye
strange	divný(-á/-é)	div-nee
strawberry	jahoda	ya-ho-da
street	ulice	oo-li-tse
street map	plán města	plan mnYes-ta
stroke	mrtvice	mrrt-vi-tse
strong (tea, coffee)	silný(-á/-é)	sil-nee
student (m/f)	student(ka)	stoo-dent(-ka)
is there a student discount?	mají studenti slevu?	ma-yi stu-den-ti sle-voo?
stuffing (for turkey, etc.)	nádivka	na-div-ka
stung	poštipaný (-á/-é)	po-shtee-pa-nee
stupid	hloupý(-á/-é)	hlow-pee
suddenly	náhle	na-hle
sugar	cukr	tsoo-krr
suit (man's)	oblek	ob-lek
suit (woman's)	kostým	kos-teem
suitcase	kufr	koo-frr
summer	léto	le-to
to sunbathe	opalovat se	o-pa-lo-vat se

sunburnt	spálený(-á/-é)	spa-le-nee(-a/-e)
sun cream	krém na opalování	krém na o-pa-lo-va-nee
Sunday	neděle	ne-dye-le
sun glasses	sluneční brýle	sloo-nech-nee bree-le
sunny	slunný(-á/-é)	sloo-nee(-a/-e)
supper	večeře	ve-che-rzhe
supplement (on Intercity train, etc.)	příplatek	przhee-pla-tek
sure	jistý(-á/-é)	yis-tee(-a/-e)
surname	příjmení	przhee-me-nee
to swear (bad language)	nadávat	na-da-vat
to sweat	potit se	po-tit-se
sweet adj	sladký(-á/-é)	slad-kee(-a/-e)
sweetener	umělé sladidlo	oo-mnye-le sla-did-lo
sweets	bonbóny	bon-bo-ni
to swim	plavat	pla-vat
swimming-pool	koupaliště	koW-pa-lish-tYe;
swimsuit	plavky	plav-ki
switch	vypínač	vi-pee-nach
to switch off	vypnout	vip-noWt
to switch on	zapnout	zap-noWt
swollen (finger, ankle, etc.)	oteklý(-á/-é)	o-tek-lee(-a/-e)
T		
table	stůl	stool
tablet (pill)	tableta	tab-le-ta
to take	vzít	vzeet
how long does it take?	jak dlouho to trvá?	yak dloW-ho to tr-va?
to talk	mluvit	mloo-vit
tall	vysoký(-á/-é)	vi-so-kee(-a/-e)
tampons	tampóny	tam-po-ni

English – Czech

English	Czech	Pronunciation
taste: can I taste some?	mohu to ochutnat?	mo-hoo to o-khoot-nat?
taste noun	chuť	khootʸ
tax	daň	danʸ
is tax included?	je to včetně daně?	ye to vchet-nʸe da-nʸe?
taxi	taxi	ta-xi
tea	čaj	chay
a cup of tea	šálek čaje	sha-lek cha-ye
herbal tea	bylinkový čaj	bi-lin-ko-vee chay
teaspoon	lžička	lzhich-ka
teeth	zuby	zoo-bi
to telephone	telefon	te-le-fon
telephone	telefonovat	te-le-fo-no-vat
telephone box	telefonní budka	te-le-fo-nee bood-ka
telephone card	telefonní karta	telefo-nee kar-ta
telephone directory	telefonní seznam	te-le-fo-nee sez-nam
television	televize	te-le-vi-ze

English	Czech	Pronunciation
to tell	říkat	rzhee-kat
temperature	teplota	tep-lo-ta
I have a temperature	mám teplotu	mam tep-lo-too
temporary	dočasný(-á/-é)	do-chas-nee (-a/-e)
than	než	nezh
thanks	dík; díky	deek; dee-ki
thank you	děkuji	dʸe-koo-yi
that (m/f/nt)	ten/ta/to	ten/ta/to
what's that?	co to je?	tso to ye?
the		see grammar
theatre	divadlo	di-vad-lo
their	jejich	ye-yikh
there (over there)	tam	tam
there is...	je... tu	ye... too
there are...	jsou... tu	ysow... too
these	tito, tyto	ti-to, ti-to
they	oni	o-ni; see grammar

thick (of soup)	hustý(-á/-é)	hoos-tee(-a/-e)
thin (of soup)	řídký(-á/-é)	zheed-kee (-a/-e)
thing	věc	vyets
to think	myslet	mis-let
I think so	myslím, že ano	mis-leem, zhe a-no
third	třetí	tzhe-tee
thirsty: I'm thirsty	mám žízeň	mam zhee-zenY
this (m/f/nt)	ten/ta/to	ten/ta/to
those	tamty	tam-ti
throat	krk	krk
through	skrz	skrz
thunderstorm	bouřka	boWzh-ka
Thursday	čtvrtek	chtvrr-tek
ticket	lístek	lees-tek
(for travel)	jízdenka	yeez-den-ka
(for admission)	vstupenka	vstoo-pen-ka
ticket collector	revizor	re-vi-zor
ticket office	pokladna	pok-lad-na
tie noun	kravata	kra-va-ta
tight: it's too tight	je to příliš těsné	ye to pzhee-lish tYes-ne
tights	punčochové kalhoty	poon-cho-kho-ve kal-ho-ti
till (until)	do	do
time	čas	chas
what time is it?	kolik je hodin?	ko-lik ye ho-din?
timetable	jízdní řád	yeezd-nee tzhad
tip (to waiter, etc.)	spropitné	spro-pit-ne
tired	unavený(-á/-é)	oo-na-ve-nee (-a/-e)
tissues: have you any tissues?	máte papírové kapesníky?	ma-te papee-ro-ve kapes-nee-ki?
to	do; na	do; na; see grammar
to London	do Londýna	do lon-dee-na

English – Czech

English	Czech	Pronunciation
to the airport	na letiště	na le-tish-tYe
toast	toust; topinka	toWst; to-pin-ka
tobacconist's	tabák	ta-bak
today	dnes	dnes
together	dohromady	do-hro-ma-di
we'll pay together	platíme dohromady	pla-tee-me do-hro-ma-di
toilet	toalety; záchod	to-ale-ti; za-khod
tomato	rajče	ray-che
tomorrow	zítra	zeet-ra
tomorrow morning	zítra ráno	zeet-ra ra-no
tongue	jazyk	ya-zik
tonic water	tonik	to-nik
tonight	dnes večer	dnes ve-cher
too	příliš	pShee-lish
too hot	příliš horko	pShee-lish hor-ko
tooth	zub	zoob
toothache	bolest zubu	bo-lest zoo-boo
toothbrush	kartáček na zuby	kar-ta-chek na zoo-bi
toothpaste	pasta na zuby	pas-ta na zoo-bi
top: the top floor	nejvyšší poschodí	ney-vi-shee pos-kho-dee
total: what's the total?	kolik to je celkem?	ko-lik to ye tsel-kem?
tough (of meat)	tvrdý(-á/-é)	tvr-dee(-a/-e)
tour	zájezd	za-yezd
tourist (m/f)	turista (turistka)	too-ris-ta (too-rist-ka)
tourist office	informace	in-for-ma-tse
tow: can you tow me?	můžete mě odtáhnout?	moo-zhe-te mnYe od-ta-hnoWt?
tower	věž	vYezh
town	město	mnYes-to
town centre	střed města	stShed mnYes-ta
town hall	radnice	rad-ni-tse

English	Czech	
toy	hračka	hrach-ka
traditional	tradiční	tra-dich-nee
traffic	doprava	dop-ra-va
traffic jam	dopravní zácpa	dop-rav-nee zats-pa
traffic lights	semafor	se-ma-for
train	vlak	vlak
tram	tramvaj	tram-vay
to translate	přeložit	přzhe-lo-zhit
to travel	cestovat	tses-to-vat
travel agency	cestovní kancelář	tses-tov-nee kan-tse-la-řzh
trip (excursion)	výlet	vee-let
trouble	problém	prob-lem
trousers	kalhoty	kal-ho-ti
true: that's true	to je pravda	to ye prav-da
that's not true	to není pravda	to ne-nee prav-da
to try	zkusit	zkoor-sit
to try on (clothes, etc.)	zkusit si	zkoo-sit si
T-shirt	tričko	trich-ko
Tuesday	úterý	oo-te-ree
to turn (in street, etc.)	zahnout	za-hnowt
to turn off (radio, light)	vypnout	vip-nowt
to turn on (radio, light)	zapnout	zap-nowt
twice	dvakrát	dvak-rat
tyre	pneumatika	pneW-ma-ti-ka
typical	typický(-á/-é)	ti-pits-kee(-a/-e)
U		
ugly	ošklivý(-á/-é)	osh-kli-vee(-a/-e)
umbrella	deštník	desht-neek
uncomfortable	nepohodlný (-á/-é)	ne-po-ho-dl-nee (-a/-e)
under	pod	pod

English – Czech

English – Czech

English	Czech	Pronunciation
underground (metro)	metro	met-ro
to understand	rozumět	ro-zoo-mnyet
I don't understand	nerozumím	ne-ro-zoo-meem
do you understand?	rozumíte?	ro-zoo-mee-te?
underwear	spodní prádlo	spod-nee prad-lo
to undress	svléknout se	svlek-nowt se
unemployed	nezaměstnaný (-á/-é)	ne-za-mnyest-na-nee(-a)
unleaded	bezolovnatý (-á/-é)	bez-olov-na-tee
petrol	benzin	ben-zeen
United Kingdom	Spojené království	spo-ye-ne kra-lovs-tvee
United States	Spojené státy	spo-ye-ne sta-ti
university	univerzita	oo-ni-ver-zi-ta
to unlock	odemknout	o-dem-knowt
to unpack (suitcases)	vybalit	vi-ba-lit
unpleasant	nepříjemný (-á/-é)	nep-rzhee-yem-nee(-a/-e)
until	do	do
unusual	neobvyklý (-á/-é)	ne-ob-vik-lee(-a/-e)
up: to get up	vstávat	vsta-vat
upstairs	nahoře; nahoru	na-ho-rzhe; na-ho-roo
urgent: it's urgent	je to naléhavé	ye to na-le-ha-ve
us (to)	nám	nam
(about)	nás	nas
(with)	námi	na-mi
to use	používat	pow-zhee-vat
useful	užitečný (-á/-é)	oo-zhi-tech-nee(-a/-e)
usual	obvyklý (-á/-é)	ob-vik-lee(-a/-e)
usually	obvykle	ob-vik-le

V			vitamin pills	vitamíny v tabletách	vi-ta-**mee**-ni v tab-le-**takh**
vacancy	volný pokoj	vol-**nee** po-koy	voice	hlas	hlas
valid	platný(-á/-é)	plat-**nee**(**-a/-e**)	voltage	napětí	na-**p'e-tee**
valuable: *it's valuable*	je to cenné	ye to tse-**ne**	to vomit	zvracet	zvra-tset
valuables	cennosti	tse-nos-ti	voucher	poukázka	poW-**kaz**-ka
VAT	DPH	ze-pe-ha			
vegetables	zelenina	ze-le-ni-na	**W**		
vegetarian (m/f)	vegetarián(ka)	ve-ge-ta-ri-yan (-ka)	to wait for	čekat na	che-kat na
very	velmi	vel-mi	waiter (m/f)	číšník (číšnice)	**cheesh**-neek (**cheesh**-ni-tse)
video cassette	videokazeta	vi-de-o-ka-ze-ta	waiting room	čekárna	che-**kar**-na
video recorder	video rekordér	vi-de-o-re-or-**der**	to wake up (oneself)	vzbudit	vzboo-dit
view	vyhlídka	vi-**hleed**-ka		vzbudit se	vzboo-dit-se
village	vesnice	ves-ni-tse	Wales	Wales	Weylz
vineyard	vinice	vi-ni-tse	walk noun	procházka	pro-**khaz**-ka
to visit	navštívit	nav-**shtee**-vit	to walk	chodit pěšky	kho-dit p'yesh-ki
visitors	návštěvníci	**nav**-sh-t'yev-nee-tsi	wall	zeď	zedy
			wallet	peněženka	pe-n'e-zhen-ka

English – Czech

English	Czech	pronunciation
to want	chtít	khteet; see GRAMMAR
I want...	chci...	khtsi...
warm	teplý(-á/-é)	tep-lee(-a/-e); see GRAMMAR
to warm up (milk, etc.)	ohřát	o-hřzhat
to wash (oneself)	umýt se	oo-meet se
where can I wash?	kde se mohu umýt?	kde se mo-hoo oo-meet?
wasp	vosa	vo-sa
watch (wrist)	hodinky	ho-din-ki
water	voda	vo-da
watermelon	meloun	me-lown
way: is this the right way to...?	jdu správně do...?	ydoo sprav-nye do...?
way in	vchod	vkhod
way out	východ	vee-khod

English	Czech	pronunciation
we	my	mi see GRAMMAR
weak (tea, coffee)	slabý(-á/-é)	sla-bee(-a/-e)
to wear (of clothes)	nosit	no-sit
weather	počasí	po-cha-see
weather forecast	předpověď počasí	přzhed-po-vyed'y po-cha-see
web page	webová stránka	we-bo-va stran-ka
Wednesday	středa	střzhe-da
week	týden	tee-den
weekday	pracovní den	pra-tsov-nee den
weekend	vikend	vee-kend
at the weekend	o vikendu	o vee-ken-doo
weight	váha	va-ha
welcome!	vítáme vás!	vee-ta-me vas!
well	dobře	dob-řzhe

want – without

English	Czech	pronunciation
well-done (meat)	dobře propečené	dob-rzhe pro-pe-che-ne
Welsh adj	velšský(-á/-é)	welsh-skee (-a/-e)
west	západ	za-pad
what	co	tso
what is it?	co to je?	tso to ye?
when?	kdy?	kdi?
where?	kde?	kde?
which?	který(-á/-é)?	kte-**ree**(-**a**/-**e**)?
while: in a while	za chvíli	za khvee-li
whipped cream	šlehačka	shle-hach-ka
white	bílý(-á/-é)	bee-**lee**(-**a**/-**e**)
who?	kdo?	kdo?
who is it?	kdo je to?	kdo ye to?
whole	celý(-á/-é)	tse-**lee**(-**a**/-**e**)
wholemeal bread	celozrnný chleba	tse-lo-zrr-nee khle-ba
whose?	čí?	chee?
why?	proč?	proch?
wide	široký(-á/-é)	shi-ro-**kee**(-**a**/-**e**)
wife	manželka	man-zhel-ka
to win	vyhrát	vi-hrat
window	okno	ok-no
(of shop)	výloha	**vee**-lo-ha
windy: it's windy	je vítr	ye **vee**-tr
wine	víno	**vee**-no
red wine	červené víno	cher-ve-**ne** **vee**-no
white wine	bílé víno	**bee**-**le** **vee**-no
wine bar	vinárna	vi-**nar**-na
wine cellar	vinný sklípek	vi-**nee** sklee-pek
wine list	vinný lístek	vi-**nee** lees-tek
winter	zima	zi-ma
with	s	s
with ice	s ledem	s le-dem
without	bez	bez

English – Czech

without milk	bez mléka	bez mle-ka	
woman	žena	zhe-na	
wonderful	krásný(-á/-é)	kras-nee(-a/-e)	
wood (substance)	dřevo	drze-vo	
(forest)	les	les	
word	slovo	slo-vo	
work noun	práce	pra-tse	
to work (function)	fungovat	foon-go-vat	
it doesn't work	nefunguje to	ne-foon-goo-ye -to	
worse	horší	hor-shee	
worth: *it's worth...*	má to cenu...	ma to tse noo...	
to wrap up	zabalit	za-ba-lit	
to write	psát	psat	
wrong	špatný(-á/-é)	shpat-nee(-a/-e)	
what's wrong?	co s tím je?	tso steem ye?	

X

x-ray noun	rentgen	rent-gen	
to x-ray	rentgenovat	rent-ge-no-vat	

Y

year	rok	rok	
5 years	pět let	pyet let	
yellow	žlutý(-á/-é)	zhloo-tee(-a/-e)	
Yellow Pages	Žluté stránky	zhloo-te stran-ki	
yes	ano	ano	
yesterday	včera	vche-ra	
yet	ještě	yesh-tye	
not yet	ještě ne	yesh-tye ne	
yoghurt	jogurt	yo-goort	
you	ty; vy	ti; vi; see GRAMMAR	
young	mladý(-á/-é)	mla-dee(-a/-e)	

your (sing. informal) (m/f/nt/)	tvůj/tvoje/ tvoje/	tvooj/tvo-ye/ tvo-ye
(plural; polite) (m/f/nt/)	váš/vaše/vaše	vash/va-she/ va-she
Z		
zoo	zoo	zo-o

Czech – English

A

a	and
adaptér m	adaptor
adresa f	address
adresa domů f	home address
ahoj	hello; hi!; bye!
ambulance f	surgery
Amerika f	America
americký (-á / -é) adj	American
anglicky	English
(-á / -é) adj	
angličtina f	English (language)
Anglie f	England
ano	yes
antikoncepce f	contraception
architektura f	architecture
auto nt	car
autobus m	bus; coach

autobusová stanice f	bus stop
autobusové nádraží nt	bus station
autokempink m	camping; caravan site
autoopravna f	garage; car repair service

B

balet m	ballet
balíček m	packet
balík m	parcel
balkón m	balcony
banka f	bank
bankomat m	cash dispenser; ATM
bankovka f	banknote
bar m	nightclub; bar
barevný (-á / -é)	coloured; in colour; colourful

barokní	Baroque
barva f	colour; dye
bas m	bass
baterie f	battery
baterka f	torch
batoh m	rucksack
bavit se	to enjoy oneself; to have a good time
bavlna f	cotton
běhat	to run
beletrie f	fiction
benzin m	petrol
benzinová pumpa f	petrol station
bez	without
bezpečný (-á / -é)	safe
bezplatný (-á / -é)	free of charge

Czech	English
běžky	cross-country skis
béžový (-á / -é)	beige
bílý (-á / -é)	white
blízko	near; close by
blok m	writing pad; block of flats
blůza f	blouse
bohoslužba f	church service
bok m	waist; side
bolavý (-á / -é)	sore; aching
bolest f	pain; ache
bolest hlavy f	headache
bolest zub f	toothache
bolest v krku f	sore throat
bolet	to hurt; to ache
bota f	shoe
bouda f	chalet; cabin; hut; kennel
bouře f	storm
brát	to take
bratr m	brother
broušené sklo nt	cut glass
brožovaný (-á / -é)	in paperback
brožura f	brochure; booklet
brýle pl	glasses; spectacles
brzda f	brake
brzdit	to brake
brzy	soon; early
březen m	March
břícho nt	stomach
budík m	alarm clock
budit	to wake up
budova f	building
bufet m	snack bar; cafeteria
bunda f	jacket; anorak
burza f	stock-exchange
bydlet	to live; to stay
byt m	flat
být	to be
C	
celní	customs
celní	customs duty
poplatek m	
celnice f	customs
celodenní	all-day; whole day
celý (-á / -é)	whole; entire; all
celý den	all day
cena f	price; cost
v ceně	included in price
ceník m	price list
cennosti pl	valuables
cenný (-á / --é)	valuable
cesta f	way; road; trip

Czech – English

Czech – English

Czech	English
cestopis m	travel book
cestování nt	travelling
cestovat	to travel
cestovní	travelling
cestovní kancelář f	travel agency
cestovní pas m	passport
cestovní výlohy pl	travel expenses
cigareta f	cigarette
církev f	church (i.e. the Catholic Church)
cizí	strange; foreign
cizina f	foreign country
cizinec m	foreigner (male)
cizojazyčný (–á / –é)	in a foreign language
clo nt	customs; duty
podléhající clu	subject to duty
beze cla	duty-free

Czech	English
co	what; which
cukrárna f	confectionery
cvičení nt	exercise; practice; training
cyklista m	cyclist

Č

Czech	English
čas m	time
časopis m	magazine; periodical; journal
část f	part; portion
často	often; frequently
Čech m	Czech (male)
Čechy	Bohemia
čekárna f	waiting room
černý (–á / –é)	black
čerpací stanice f	petrol station

Czech	English
čerstvý (–á / –é)	fresh
červen m	June
červenec m	July
červený (–á / –é)	red
Češka f	Czech (female)
Česká republika f	Czech Republic
český (–á / –é) adj	Czech; Bohemian
čeština f	Czech (language)
činohra f	play; drama
číslo nt	number
č. abbr	number (formal letter)
číst	to read
čistit	to clean
čisticí prostředek m	detergent
čistírna f	dry-cleaner's

Czech	English	Czech	English	Czech	English
čistý(-á/-é)	clean	datum narození nt	date of birth	dětský(-á/-é)	child's; children's; baby's
číšník m	waiter	datum vydání nt	date of issue	dětský lékař m	paediatrician
člověk m	man; person	dávat	to give	děvče nt	girl
člun m	boat (small)	dávat si pozor	to be careful	devět	nine
motorový člun	motorboat	dávka f	dose; ratio	dieta f	diet
čtrnáct dní	fortnight	dávno	long ago	mít dietu	to be on a diet
čtvrt f	quarter	dcera f	daughter	díl m	portion; share part
čtvrtek m	Thursday	deka f	blanket	náhradní díl m	spare part
čtyřhra f	doubles (in tennis, etc.)	děkovat	to thank	dílo nt	work
		děkuji vám	thank you	umělecké dílo	work of art
D		dělat	to make; to do	diskotéka f	disco
dále!	come in!	délka f	length	dítě nt	child; baby
daleko	a long way; far	den m	day	divadlo nt	theatre
dálnice f	motorway	denně adj	daily	divadelní hra f	play
další	next; following	deset	ten	dívat se	to look at; to watch
dámský(-á/-é)	lady's	desetikoruna f	ten-crown coin	dívka f	girl
dámy	ladies (toilet)	déšť m	rain	dlouhý(-á/-é)	long; tall
dárek m	present; gift	deštník m	umbrella	dnes	today
datum nt	date (day)				

Czech – English

Czech – English

Czech	English
dnes ráno	this morning
dnes večer	tonight
do	to; into; in; until; by
do Prahy	to Prague
dobrou chuť!	enjoy your meal!
dobrý(-á/-é)	good
dobrý den	hello
dobře	well
dočasný(-á/-é)	temporary
dočasná stanice f	temporary stop
dočasně	temporarily not in service
zrušen	
dohromady	altogether
doklad m	document; receipt
doktor(ka) m/f	doctor
doleva	to the left
dole	down
doma	at home
domácí m/f	landlord; landlady
donést	to bring
dopis m	letter
dopoledne	morning; in the morning
doprava	to the right
doprava f	transport
dospělý(-á/-é)	adult; grown-up
dost	enough
doutník m	cigar
dovnitř	inside
dovolená f	holiday; day off
DPH	VAT
dráha f	course; track; railway
lyžařská dráha f	ski track; ski run
drahokam m	gem; precious stone
drahý(-á/-é)	expensive; dear
drobné pl	small change
nechte si drobné	keep the change
drogerie f	shop selling toiletries
druh m	sort; type; kind
dřevo nt	wood
dřevěná hračka f	wooden toy
duben m	April
důležitý(-á/-é)	important
dům m	house
dva	two
dvakrát	twice
dveře pl	door
dvoulůžkový pokoj m	double room

E

Czech	English
elektřina f	electricity

Czech – English

Czech	English
elektrický proud m	electric current
e-mailová adresa f	e-mail address
evropský (-á/-é)	European
F	
fax m	fax
festival m	festival
filmový festival	film festival
fialový (-á/-é)	violet; purple
film m	film
celovečerní film m	feature film
kreslený film m	cartoon
formulář m	form
vyplnit formulář	to fill in a form
fotbal m	football
fotbalový zápas m	football match
fotoaparát m	camera
fotografie f	photo
barevná fotografie f	colour photo
fotografovat	to take photos
fungovat	to function; to work
G	
galerie f	art gallery
gotický (-á/-é)	Gothic
H	
hal. f	abbrev. of half
hala f	hall; corridor; lounge
haló?	hello? (on telephone)
hasicí přístroj m	fire-extinguisher
havárie f	breakdown; crash; accident
havarijní pojištění nt	general accident insurance
helma f	helmet
hezký (-á/-é)	pretty; nice; good-looking
hlad m	hunger
hlava f	head
hledat	to look for
hluk m	noise
hlučný (-á/-é)	noisy; loud
hnědý (-á/-é)	brown
hodina f	hour
kolik je hodin?	what's the time?
hodinky pl	watch
hodiny pl	clock

Czech – English

Czech	English
hodně	very; a lot; much
hodný(-á/-é)	good; worthy of
holení *nt*	shaving
holičství *nt*	barber's
hora *f*	mountain
horečka *f*	fever
horký(-á/-é)	hot
horský	mountain
horská služba *f*	mountain rescue service
hořet	to burn; to blaze
hoří!	fire!
hořký(-á/-é)	bitter
hospoda *f*	pub
host *m*	guest
hotel *m*	hotel
hotový(-á/-é)	ready
housle *pl*	violin
hra *f*	play; game
hračka *f*	toy
hrad *m*	castle
hranice *f*	frontier; border
hraniční přechod *m*	border crossing
hrát	to play; to perform
hrnek *m*	cup; mug
hrozný(-á/-é)	awful; terrible
hrtan *m*	throat
hřbitov *m*	cemetery
hudba *f*	music

CH

Czech	English
chalupa *f*	cottage; hut
chata *f*	hut; cottage
chirurg *m*	surgeon
chlapec *m*	boy; boyfriend
chodba *f*	corridor; passage; hall
chodit	to go; to walk
chodník *m*	pavement
chrám *m*	cathedral; church
chrup *m*	teeth
umělý chrup *m*	dentures
chřipka *f*	influenza; flu
chtít	to want
chuť *f*	taste; flavour; appetite
chyba *f*	mistake; error; fault
chybět	to miss; to be absent

I

Czech	English
igelit *m*	plastic
ihned	at once; immediately
infarkt *m*	heart attack
infekce *f*	infection
infekční	infectious
nemoc *f*	disease

Czech – English

informace f — information
informovat se — to ask for information
injekce f — injection
internetová kavárna — Internet café
inzerát m — advertisement
Ir(ka) — Irishman (woman)
Irsko nt — Ireland
irský(-á/-é) adj — Irish

J

já — I
jak — how
jako — as; like
jaký — what, which
jaro nt — spring (season)
jazyk m — language
jeden — one

jednosměrná ulice f — one-way street
jedovatý (-á/-é) — poisonous
jemný(-á/-é) — fine; soft; delicate
jet — to go; to travel
...jede jen do stanice... — ...terminates at...
jezero nt — lake
jídelní vůz m — dining car
jídlo nt — food; meal; dish
jih — south
jiný(-á/-é) — other; another; different
jíst — to eat
jít — to go; to walk
jízdenka f — ticket (for bus, train, etc.)
jízdní řád m — timetable
jméno nt — name

křestní jméno nt — first name
rodné jméno nt — maiden name; née

K

k — to; towards; for
kabát m — coat
kabelka f — handbag
kadeřnictví nt — hairdresser's
kalhotky pl — knickers, briefs
kalhoty pl — trousers
kam — where
kamarád(ka) m/f — friend

kamera f — video-camera
Kanada — Canada
kanadský (-á/-é) — Canadian

kancelář f — office

Czech – English

Czech	English
cestovní kancelář f	travel agency
kapesní	pocket
kapesník m	handkerchief
kapsa f	pocket
kapsář m	pick-pocket
karanténa f	quarantine
karát m	carat
karosérie f	body (car)
karta f	card
kartáček na zuby m	toothbrush
kašel m	cough
kašna f	fountain
katedrála f	cathedral
kavárna f	café
každý (-á / -é)	every; each
Kč	abbr. of koruna
kde	where
kdo	who
kdy	when
kino nt	cinema
klavír m	piano
klenoty pl	jewellery
klíč m	key
klimatizace f	air-conditioning
klobása f	sausage
kluzký (-á / -é)	slippery
kluziště nt	skating rink
kniha f	book
knihkupectví nt	bookshop
knihovna f	library; bookcase
koberec m	carpet
kočka f	cat
kolej f	rail; hostel
kolek m	stamp (for tax)
kolik?	how much?; how many?
kolo nt	wheel; bicycle
koncert m	concert
konečná stanice f	terminus
kontaktní čočky pl	contact lenses
konto nt	account
konvice f	pot; kettle
konzerva f	tin; can
kopec m	hill
kopie f	copy
koruna f	crown (Czech / Slovak currency)
kořeněný (-á / -é)	spicy; seasoned
kostel m	church
košile f	shirt
noční košile f	nightdress
koupaliště nt	swimming pool
koupelna f	bathroom
koupit	to buy
kouření nt	smoking

kouření zakázáno no smoking
kousek *m* piece; bit
kožešnictví *nt* furrier's
krabice *f* box; case
krádež *f* theft
krajina *f* scenery; countryside
krásný(-á/-é) beautiful; wonderful
krátký(-á/-é) short; brief
kreditní karta *f* credit card
krev *f* blood
krevní skupina *f* blood group
kruhový objezd *m* roundabout
krvácet to bleed
křen *m* horse-radish
křižovatka *f* crossing
který(-á/-é) what; which

kufr *m* suitcase
kuchařka *f* cook (*female*); cookery book
kuchyně *f* kitchen; cuisine
kůň *m* horse
kupé *nt* compartment (*on train*)
kurs *m* exchange rate
kůže *f* leather; skin
květen *m* May
květina *f* flower
květinářství *nt* florist's
kyvadlová doprava *f* shuttle bus

L

lahev *f* bottle
lahůdky delicatessen
lanovka *f* cable railway; funicular

lázně *pl* public baths; spa
léčit to treat; to cure
leden *m* January
lednička *f* fridge
lehátkový vůz sleeping car
lék *m* medicine; drug
lék proti bolesti *m* painkiller
lékárna *f* pharmacy
lékárnička *f* first-aid kit
lékař(ka) *m/f* doctor
všeobecný lékař *m* general practitioner
zubní lékař dentist
lékařská prohlídka *f* check up
lékařský předpis *m* prescription
lepidlo *nt* glue
lepší better

Czech – English

Czech	English
les *m*	wood; forest
let *m*	flight
letadlo *nt*	plane
letecky	by air mail
letenka *f*	air ticket
letiště *nt*	airport
léto *nt*	summer
letuška *f*	flight attendant
levný(-á/-é)	cheap
levý(-á/-é)	left
libra *f*	pound
lidé *pl*	people
lidová řemesla *pl*	country crafts
listopad *m*	November
listovní zásilky *pl*	letters; postcards; mail
litr *m*	litre
loď *f*	ship; boat
Londýn *m*	London
loutka *f*	puppet
lůžkový vůz *m*	sleeping car
lyžařský(-á/-é)	ski-
lyžařské boty *pl*	ski boots
lyžařské hole *pl*	ski poles
lyžařské vybavení *nt*	ski equipment
lyžařský vlek *m*	ski lift
lyže *f*	skis
lyžovat	to ski
lžíce *f*	spoon
lžička	teaspoon

M

Czech	English
malíř *m*	painter
malířství *nt*	painting
málo	little; a few
malovat	to paint; to decorate
malý(-á/-é)	small; little
máma *f*	mummy
manžel *m*	husband
manželka *f*	wife
mapa *f*	map
mast *f*	ointment
měna *f*	currency
méně	less
menstruační vložky *pl*	sanitary towels
menší	smaller; lesser
měsíc *m*	moon; month
jednou za měsíc	once a month
město *nt*	town; city
Hlavní město *nt*	capital
metro *nt*	underground; metro
mezinárodní	international
jízdenky	tickets
MHD *f*	public transport
milovat	to love

milý(-á/-é) dear; nice; pleasant
mimo except
mimo pondělí except Monday
mince f coin
minulý(-á/-é) last; previous
místenka f seat reservation
místní local
místnost f room
místo nt room; place; spot
mít to have; to possess
mít raději to prefer
mladý(-á/-é) young
mluvit to speak; to talk
mnoho much; many; a lot of
množství nt quantity; amount
móda f fashion; style

modrý(-á/-é) blue
Morava f Moravia
moravský (-á/-é) Moravian
most m bridge
motocykl m motorcycle
motor m motor; engine
motorový člun m motor boat
moucha f fly
mše f mass
můj my; mine
muset to have to
muzeum nt museum
muzikál m musical
muž m man; male
muži gents (toilet)
my we; us
mýdlo nt soap
myslet to think

N

na on; to; at
zastávka na znamení request stop
nabízet to offer
nabízíme... we offer...
nábřeží nt embankment quay (formal letter)
nábř. abbr.
nábytek m furniture
nachlazení cold (illness)
nad above; over
nadjezd m overhead crossing; flyover
nádraží nt railway station
nadúrovňová křižovatka f flyover
nafta f oil; diesel
nahoru upstairs; up

Czech – English

Czech	English
náhrada *f*	compensation; refund
náhradní díl *m*	spare part
náhubek *m*	muzzle
nájem *m*	hire; rent; lease
nakažlivý (-á/-é)	infectious
náměstí *nt*	square
nám. *abbr.*	square *(formal letter)*
náplast *f*	plaster
naproti	opposite
např.	e.g.
národní	national
národnost *f*	nationality
narození *nt*	birth
narozeniny *pl*	birthday
nastoupit do vlaku	to board *(a train)*
nástupiště *nt*	platform
naučná stezka *f*	nature trail
návštěvenka *f*	visiting card; card
ne	no; not
nebezpečný (-á/-é)	dangerous
na vlastní nebezpečí	at one's own risk
něco	something
neděle *f*	Sunday
nedělní prodej *m*	open on Sunday
nehoda *f*	accident
nejlepší	best
nemocnice *f*	hospital
nemocný (-á/-é)	ill; sick
neplatný (-á/-é)	not valid
neprůjezdná oblast	closed to traffic
nepřestupný tarif *m*	single journey only
nevyplňujte prosím	please leave blank
nic	nothing
nikdo	nobody
nikdy	never
noc *f*	night
celou noc	all night
nosnost *f*	maximum load
nouzový východ *m*	emergency exit
noviny *pl*	newspaper
nový (-á/-é)	new
nula *f*	zero; nought; nil
nůž *m*	knife
nyní	now; at present

O

Czech	English
o	about; of; at
o vánocich	at Christmas
oba	both
oběd *m*	lunch; dinner
obědvat	to have lunch
obchod *m*	shop; business
obchodní dům *m*	department store
objížďka *f*	diversion
oblast *f*	region; area
oblečení *nt*	clothes
obraz *m*	picture
obsazeno	engaged (*phone, etc.*); full; occupied
obsah *m*	contents; plot; volume
obuv *f*	footwear
obyvací pokoj *m*	living room

Czech	English
očkování *nt*	vaccination
oční lékař(ka) *m/f*	oculist
od... do	from ... to
odbočka *f* doprava *f*	turning to the right
oddělení *nt*	department; ward
oddělení ztrát a nálezů *nt*	lost and found office
odejit	to go away; to leave (*on foot*)
odjet	to leave (*by means of transport*)
odjezd *m*	departure (*by train, bus*)
odlet *m*	departure (*by plane*)
odpadky *pl*	litter; rubbish

Czech	English
odpoledne *nt*	afternoon; in the afternoon
oheň *m*	fire
okno *nt*	window
oko *nt*	eye
okolí *nt*	neighbourhood
okružní jízda *f*	tour
okružní plavba lodí *f*	sightseeing cruise
omezení rychlosti *nt*	speed limit
on	he; it
ona	she; it; they
oni	they
opalovat se	to sunbathe
opravna hodinek *f*	watch repairer's
optika *f*	optician's
ordinace *f*	surgery
ordinační hodiny *pl*	surgery hours

Czech – English

Czech – English

orloj m	astronomical clock
osoba f	person
osobně	personally
osobní vlak m	passenger train
otázka f	question
otec m	father
otevřeno	open
otevřít	to open
otevírací doba f	opening hours
otvírák na konzervy m	tin opener
otvírák na láhve m	bottle opener
označte si jízdenku	punch your ticket

P

pacient m	patient
padat	to fall
palác m	palace
památka f	souvenir; monument
pán m	man; Mr; gentleman
p. abbr.	Mr (formal letter)
pánské slipy pl	men's briefs
paní f	woman; Mrs; madam; wife
pí abbr.	Mrs (formal letter)
páni pl	gents (toilet)
pantomima f	mime
papír m	paper
pár m	pair; couple
paragon m	receipt
pardon!	sorry; excuse me!
park m	park
parkovací hodiny pl	parking meter
parkování zakázáno	no parking
parkoviště nt	car park
parník m	steamboat
pas m	passport
pásek m	seat belt
pás m	belt; tape
pásmo nt	zone
pasová kontrola f	passport control
pátek m	Friday
patro nt	floor; storey
pěkný(-á/-é)	nice; fine; pretty
peněženka f	purse
peníze pl	money
penzion m	guesthouse
permanentka f	season ticket
pero nt	pen; feather
pes m	dog
pět	five
pěvecký sbor m	choir

Czech	English
písek *m*	sand
píseň *f*	song
pít	to drink
pitná voda *f*	drinking water
pivovar *m*	brewery
placka *f*	thick pancake
platit	to pay
platit v hotovosti	to pay in cash
platný(-á/-é)	valid
platnost končí...	expires...
plavat	to swim
plavání zakázáno	no swimming
plavecký bazén *m*	swimming pool
plavky *pl*	swimsuit
plechovka *f*	tin; can
plomba *f*	filling (*for tooth*)
plnoletý(-á/-é)	of age
plyn *m*	gas
po	after; about; over;
po ulici	along the street
pobočka *f*	branch (*office*)
počasí *nt*	weather
počítač *m*	computer
pod	under; below
podchod *m*	subway
podjezd *m*	underpass
podnik *m*	firm; enterprise
podnikatel *m*	businessman; entrepreneur
podpis *m*	signature
podzim *m*	autumn
pohled *m*	view, postcard
pohraničí *nt*	border area
pojistit	to insure
pojištění *nt*	insurance
pojišťovna *f*	insurance company
pokladna *f*	booking office; box office
pokoj *m*	room
pokojská *f*	chambermaid
pokračovat	to continue
pokuta *f*	fine; penalty
poledne *nt*	noon; midday
polední přestávka *f*	lunch break
policejní stanice *f*	police station
policie *f*	police
poliklinika *f*	health centre
pomalu	slowly
pomalý(-á/-é)	slow
pomazánka *f*	spread
pomeranč *m*	orange
pomerančový džem *m*	orange marmalade
pomník *m*	monument
pomoc *f*	help; assistance

Czech – English

Czech	English
pondělí nt	Monday
ponožky pl	socks
poplatek m	charge; fee
porcelán m	china; porcelain
poschodí nt	floor
poslat poštou	to send by post
poslední	last; latest
poslouchat	to listen to
postel f	bed
pošta f	post office
poštovní schránka f	letter-box
potok m	stream
potrava f	food
potraviny pl	grocer's
potřeby pro domácnost	household goods
potvrzení nt	receipt
pouze	only
použitý(-á/-é)	used, second-hand
povolání nt	occupation
povolení nt	licence
jen pro držitele povolení	licence holders only
povolení k pobytu nt	residence permit
poznámky pl	notes; comments
poznávací značka f	car number-plate
pozor m	attention; beware of
pozvání nt	invitation
požár m	fire
požární poplach m	fire alarm
práce f	work
pracovní doba f	working hours
pracovní povolení nt	work permit
pradlenka	laundrette
prádlo nt	underwear; (washing) laundry
Praha	Prague
do Prahy	to Prague
v Praze	in Prague
pravda f	truth
pravidlo nt	rule
pravý(-á/-é)	right; real; true
prázdný (-á/-é)	empty; vacant
prezervativ m	condom
pro	for; because of
proclít	to declare (for customs); to clear customs
proč	why
prodat	to sell
prodej m	sale
program m	programme

Czech	English
prohlídka f	sightseeing; visit
pronajmout si	to rent
prosinec m	December
prosím	please; excuse me; you're welcome!
proti	opposite; against; for
lék proti nachlazení	medicine for a cold
protože	because; since
provádět	to show round
provoz m	traffic
prozatimní	temporary
prst m	finger
pršet	to rain
průchod m	passage (for pedestrians)
průjem m	diarrhoea
průjezd m	way through (for vehicles)
průkaz m	identity card; pass card
řidičský průkaz m	driving licence
průsmyk m	pass
průvodce m	guide (person); guidebook
první	first
první pomoc f	first aid
pryč	away; off; gone
přání nt	wish; wishes
před	before; outside; in front of
předčíslí nt	dialling code
předem	in advance; beforehand
předjíždění nt	overtaking
přední	front
předpis m	recipe; prescription
předpověď f / předpověď	forecast
předpověď počasí f	weather forecast
předprodej m	advance booking
přechod pro chodce m	crossing
přechodný (-á/-é)	temporary
přejezd m	crossing; level crossing
přejít ulici	to cross the street
překročení rychlosti	speeding
přes	over; across
přes noc	overnight
přesedat	to change (trains)

Czech – English

Czech – English

přestávka f	intermission; interval; break	příplatek m	extra charge, supplement
přestože	although	připravený (-á / -é)	ready
přestup na...	change for... (train, tram)	příroda f	nature; countryside
přestupek m	offence	přírodní	natural
příbor m	knife and fork; cutlery	příručka f	handbook; manual
přihláška f	application form	přistání nt	landing (of plane)
příchod m	arrival	přístup k hotelu m	access to the hotel
příjezd m	arrival	příští	next; following
přijít	to arrive	přítel m	friend (male); boyfriend
příjmení nt	surname	přítelkyně f	friend (female); girlfriend
přílet m	arrival (by plane)	přívěs m	caravan; trailer
přiletět	to arrive (by plane)	přízemí nt	ground floor
příliš	too	psát	to write
přímo	direct; straight		
přímý let m	direct flight		
přímý vlak m	through train		

ptát se	to ask		
půjčovna f	rental shop; for hire		
půl	half		
půlnoc f	midnight		
R			
rameno nt	shoulder		
ráno nt	morning		
v pondělí ráno	on Monday morning		
rasismus m	racism		
razítko nt	rubber stamp		
recepce f	reception		
recepční	receptionist		
recept m	prescription; recipe		
reklama f	advertisement		
reklamace f	claim		
rekreační oblast f	holiday resort		

Czech	English
renesanční	Renaissance
reprodukce f	print
restaurace f	restaurant
revizor m/f	inspector
režie f	direction
robot m	robot; food processor
ročně	annually
ročník m	volume; class; vintage
rodiče pl	parents
rodilý m	native (speaker)
rodina f	family
roh m	horn; corner
na rohu	on the corner
rok m	year
v příštím roce	next year
Šťastný Nový rok!	Happy New Year!
rokokový (-á/-é)	rococo (in architecture)
Rom(ka) m/f	Romany (person), Roma, Gypsy
román m	novel
románský (-á/-é)	Romance; Romanesque
rostlina f	plant
rozcestí n	crossroads
rozhlas m	radio
rozumět	to understand
rozvedený(-á)	divorced
RTG m	X-ray
ruční práce	hand-made
ruční m	towel
ruka f	hand
rukavice f	glove
rušný (-á/-é)	busy
růžový(-á/-é)	pink; rose
rybářský lístek m	fishing permit
rybářský prut m	fishing rod
rychle	fast; quickly
rychlík m	fast/express train
rychloopravna f	repairs while-you-wait
rychlost f	speed; gear
rychlý(-á/-é)	quick; fast
rýma f	cold (illness)
dostat rýmu	to catch a cold

Ř

Czech	English
řada f	row (line)
řeč f	language; speech
ředitel m	director; headmaster; manager
ředkvička f	radish
řeka f	river

Czech – English

řetízek – spropitné

Czech	English
řetízek *m*	chain
řezané pivo *nt*	mixture of light and dark beer
řeznictví *nt*	butcher's
říci	to say
řidič(ka) *m/f*	driver
řidičský průkaz *m*	driving licence
říjen *m*	October

S

Czech	English
s	with
sáček *m*	bag
sada *f*	set
sako *nt*	jacket; blazer
sál *m*	hall
sám	alone; by oneself
sanitka *f*	ambulance
sauna *f*	sauna
secesní	Art Nouveau
sedadlo *nt*	seat
sedm	seven
semafor *m*	traffic lights
servírka *f*	waitress
sestra *f*	sister; nurse
setkání *nt*	meeting
sever *m*	north
seznam *m*	list
sezóna *f*	season
schod *m*	stair; step
po schodech dolů	downstairs
po schodech nahoru	upstairs
schodiště *nt*	staircase
silnice *f*	road
Silvestr *m*	New Year's Eve
sjízdný(-á/-é)	passable; open
sklenice *f*	glass
sklo *nt*	glass (substance)
skříňka *f*	box
skříňka na zavazadla *f*	locker
skupina *f*	group
slavnost *f*	festival; celebration
slavnostní	festive
slečna *f*	young woman; Miss
sl. *abbr.*	Miss (formal letter)
sleva *f*	reduction; discount
slipy *pl*	briefs; underpants
slovanský	Slavic; Slavonic
Slovák *m* (-á/-é)	Slovak (man)
Slovensko *nt*	Slovakia
slovenský (-á/-é)	Slovak

slovenština *f* — Slovak (language)
slovník *m* — dictionary
naučný slovník m — encyclopedia
slovo *nt* — word
složenka *f* — postal order
sluchátko *nt* — receiver (telephone)
slunce *nt* — sun
služba *f* — service
směnárna *f* — bureau de change, exchange office
směr *m* — direction
směrem k... — in the direction of...
směrovací číslo *nt* — postcode
směrovka *f* — indicator

smím — I can; I may
nesmím — I mustn't
smlouva *f* — contract
snadný(-á/-é) — easy
sněhová závěj *f* — snow drift
sněhové řetězy *pl* — snow chains
sněžit — to snow
sníh *m* — snow
snížení cen *nt* — price reduction
sobota *f* — Saturday
socha *f* — statue; sculpture
soubor *m* — collection; set
současný (-á/-é) — contemporary; modern
součástka *f* — part
součet *m* — sum; total
soukromý (-á/-é) — private

souprava končí ve stanici... — train terminates at... *(metro)*
sourozenci *pl* — brothers and sisters; siblings
soutěska *f* — pass
spací pytel *m* — sleeping bag
spací vůz *m* — sleeping car
spát — to sleep
spodní — bottom, lower
spodní prádlo *nt* — underwear
spoj *m* — connection
spolu — together
sportovní hala *f* — indoor sports stadium
správce *m* — manager; administrator
sprcha *f* — shower
spropitné *nt* — tip *(in restaurant)*

Czech – English

Czech - English

Czech	English
srpen m	August
stadión m	stadium
stálý(-á / -é)	permanent
stan m	tent
stánek m	stall; kiosk
stanice f	stop (bus, tram, etc.)
stanoviště taxíků nt	taxi rank
starožitnictví nt	antique shop
starý(-á / -é)	old
státní	state
stěna f	wall
stezka f	path; trail
sto	hundred
století nt	century
strava f	food; diet
stroj m	machine
strom m	tree
strop m	ceiling
středa f	Wednesday
stříbrný(-á / -é)	silver
stůl m	table
stupeň m	grade; degree
suterén m	basement
svátek m	festival; holiday; nameday
svatý(-á / -é)	holy; saint
svět m	world
světlo nt	light
svetr m	sweater
syn m	son
synagoga f	synagogue

Š
Czech	English
šálek m	cup
šálek čaje	cup of tea
šatna f	cloakroom
šaty pl	dress
šedivý(-á / -é)	grey
šek m	cheque
šest	six
široký(-á / -é)	wide
škoda f	damage; harm; pity
škola f	school
šortky pl	shorts (trousers)
špatně	badly; wrong
špatný(-á / -é)	bad
šperk m	jewel
špinavý(-á / -é)	dirty
šťastný(-á / -é)	happy; lucky
Šťastnou cestu!	have a good trip!
Štědrý den m	Christmas Eve
štěstí nt	happiness; good luck

T
Czech	English
ta f	this
tabák m	tobacconist's
tableta f	tablet; pill
tábořiště nt	campsite

Czech	English
tak	so
talíř m	plate
tampóny pl	tampons
taška f	bag; satchel
taxi nt	taxi
těhotenství nt	pregnancy
tekoucí horká a studená voda	hot and cold running water
telefon m	telephone
telefonní karta f	phonecard
telefonní seznam m	telephone directory
telefonovat	to phone
televize f	television
tělocvična f	gym
ten	this
tenisový kurt m	tennis court
termoska f	flask
těžký(-á/-é)	heavy; difficult
tisíc m	thousand
tlak krve m	blood pressure
tlumočit	to interpret
tmavý(-á/-é)	dark
to nt	this
toaletní papír m	toilet paper
toalety pl	toilets
tradice f	tradition
tramvaj f	tram
trasa f	line (metro); route
trh m	market
tričko nt	T-shirt
trolejbus m	trolleybus
tržnice f	indoor market
tři	three
třikrát	three times
tunel m	tunnel
turista m	tourist
turistická ubytovna f	hostel
tužka f	pencil
tvrdý(-á/-é)	hard; heavy
týden m	week
tykat si	to address each other using the familiar form

U

Czech	English
u	near; close; by; with
u nás	at our place
ubytování nt	accommodation
učitel(ka) m/f	teacher
ukázat	to show
ukazatel m	signpost
ulice f	street
ul. abbr.	street (formal letter)

Czech – English

Czech	English
umělecko-průmyslové muzeum *nt*	museum of applied arts
umění *nt*	art
umět	to be able to do; to know
unavený (-á/-é)	tired
únor *m*	February
úraz *m*	accident; injury
úřad *m*	office
úřední	official
hodiny pl	business hours
úschovna zavazadel *f*	left-luggage office
úterý *nt*	Tuesday
uzavřený (-á/-é)	closed
silnice je uzavřena	the road is closed

Czech	English
úzký (-á/-é)	narrow
V	
v	in; at; on
v březnu	in March
v poledne	at noon
v sobotu	on Saturday
vadný (-á/-é)	defective
vagón *m*	carriage; coach
Vánoce *pl*	Christmas
o vánocích	at Christmas
Veselé Vánoce!	Merry Christmas!
vánoční	
stromeček *m*	Christmas tree
vařit	to cook
váš	your; yours
vata *f*	cotton wool
včera	yesterday
včetně	including; included

Czech	English
vdaná	married (of woman)
věc *f*	thing; matter; cause
večer *nt*	evening; in the evening
dnes večer	tonight
zítra večer	tomorrow night
vědět	to know
vedle	beside; next to
vedoucí *m/f*	manager
vegetarián *m*	vegetarian
věk *m*	age
velice	very; greatly
Velikonoce	Easter
velikonoční pomlázka *f*	Easter carolling whip (part of a Czech Easter folk custom)
velikost *f*	size
velký (-á/-é)	big; large

Czech	English
velmi	very
velmi mnoho	very much
velvyslanectví *nt*	embassy
ven	out
venku	outdoor; in the open air
ventil *m*	valve
ventilace *f*	ventilation
veřejný(-á/-é)	public
veřejné záchodky pl	public toilets
vesnice *f*	village
vchod *m*	entrance
vidět	to see
vidlička *f*	fork
vikend *m*	weekend
vinárna *f*	wine bar
vizitka *f*	visiting card; business card
vjezd *m*	drive; gateway
vlak *m*	train
vlažný(-á/-é)	lukewarm
vléct	to tow
vlečné lano *nt*	tow rope
vlek *m*	ski lift
vlevo	on/to the left
vlhký(-á/-é)	damp
vlněný(-á/-é)	woollen
vložky *pl*	sanitary towels
voda *f*	water
vodník *m*	water-sprite
vodopád *m*	waterfall
volant *m*	steering wheel
volno *nt*	spare/free/leisure time
volný(-á/-é)	free; loose; vacant
volné místo *nt*	vacancy
vozidlo *nt*	vehicle
vozidlo v protisměru	oncoming vehicle
vozovka *f*	road
vpravo	on/to the right
vrátnice *f*	porter's lodge; reception
vrátný *m*	porter; security guard
vrchní	top; upper
vstup *m*	entry; entrance
vstup volný m	admission free
vstup zakázán m	no entry
vstupenka *f*	ticket (for cinema, theatre, etc.)
vstupné nt	admission
dobrovolné	voluntary contribution
všechno nt	all; everything
všechno nejlepší k narozeninám	many happy returns!

vteřina f — second
vy — you (plural or polite form)
výborný(-á/-é) — excellent
výčep m — tap-room
výdej m — issue; collection point
východ m — exit; east
vypínač m — switch
vyplnit — to fill in
vyprodáno — sold out
výprodej m — clearance; sale
vypršet — to expire
vysoký(-á/-é) — high
vysoká škola f — university; college
výstup m — exit (metro, tram, bus)
vyšetření nt — examination; check-up
výtah m — lift

vývrtka f — corkscrew
vyzvednout — to claim (luggage)
vzduch m — air
vzít — to take
vzkaz m — message
vždy — always

W

webová stránka f — web page

Z

z — from; out of
za — behind; beyond
za týden — in a week
zabalit — to wrap up
začít — to start; to begin
záda pl — back
zadarmo — free of charge

zadek m — bottom; buttocks
zadní — back
zahrada f — garden
zahradní restaurace f — garden restaurant
zahraniční — foreign
záchod m — toilet; WC
zájezd m — excursion; trip
zajímavý (-á/-é) — interesting
zákaz — ban; prohibition
zákaz předjíždění — no overtaking
záloha f — deposit
zámek m — mansion; castle, lock
zánět m — inflammation
západ m — west
zápalky pl — matches

Czech	English
zápas m	fight; match; contest
fotbalový zápas m	football match
záruční lhůta f	guarantee
záruční list m	certificate of guarantee
září nt	September
zastávka f	stop
zastávka na znamení f	request stop
zastávka dočasně zrušena	stop temporarily out of service
zatáčka f	bend; curve
zátka f	cork
závada f	defect
zavazadlo nt	luggage
zavírací doba f	closing time
zavřeno	closed (sign)
zboží nt	goods
zdarma	free of charge
zde	here
zdraví nt	health
na zdraví	cheers!
zdravotní středisko nt	health centre
zeď f	wall
zelený(-á/-é)	green
země f	country
zima f	winter; cold
zimní	winter sports
stadion m	stadium
zítra	tomorrow
zlato nt	gold
zlevnění nt	price reduction
zlý(-á/-é)	bad; evil
známka f	stamp; sign
znát	to know
zóna f	zone
zoologická zahrada f	zoo
zpáteční jízdenka f	return ticket
zpoždění nt	delay
zrušit	to cancel; to call off
ztráta f	loss
zub m	tooth
zubař m	dentist
zubní pasta f	toothpaste
zvěrolékař m	vet
zvíře nt	animal

Ž

Czech	English
žádat	to ask for
žádný(-á/-é)	no
žádný autobus m	no bus
žampión m	champignons
žehlička f	iron (for ironing)
žena f	woman; female; wife

ženatý	married (of man)
ženy pl	ladies' (toilet)
Žid(ovka) m/f	Jew
židovský (-á/-é)	Jewish
žít	to live
život m	life
životní	the
prostředí nt	environment
žízeň f	thirst
žlutý (-á/-é)	yellow

Further titles in Collins' phrasebook range
Collins Gem Phrasebook

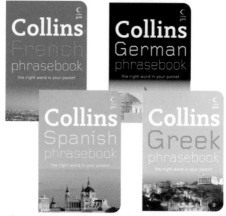

Also available as **Phrasebook CD Pack**
Other titles in the series

Collins Phrasebook & Dictionary

Also available as **Phrasebook CD Pack**
Other titles in the series
German Japanese Portuguese Spanish

Collins Easy: Photo Phrasebook

Also available as
**Phrasebook
CD Pack**

**Other titles
in the series**
Easy French
Easy Greek
Easy Italian

To order any of these titles, please telephone
0870 787 1732. For further information about all
Collins books, visit our website: www.collins.co.uk